WILLIAMS-SONOMA

Soup for Supper

GENERAL EDITOR

Chuck Williams

RECIPES

Joyce Goldstein

PHOTOGRAPHY

Richard Eskite

TIME
LIFE
BOOKS

TIME-LIFE BOOKS

Time-Life Books is a division of Time Life Inc.
Time-Life is a trademark of Time Warner Inc. U.S.A

TIME-LIFE CUSTOM PUBLISHING
Vice President and Publisher: Terry Newell
Managing Editor: Donia Ann Steele
Director of Acquisitions: Jennifer L. Pearce
Vice President of Sales and Marketing: Neil Levin
Director of Financial Operations: J. Brian Birky

WILLIAMS-SONOMA
Founder and Vice Chairman: Chuck Williams
Book Buyer: Victoria Kalish

WELDON OWEN INC.
President: John Owen
Vice President and Publisher: Wendely Harvey
Chief Operating Officer: Larry Partington
Vice President International Sales: Stuart Laurence
Associate Publisher: Lisa Atwood
Managing Editor: Jan Newberry
Consulting Editor: Norman Kolpas
Copy Editor: Sharon Silva
Design: Kari Perin, Perin+Perin
Production Director: Stephanie Sherman
Production Manager: Jen Dalton
Production Editor: Sarah Lemas
Food Stylist: George Dolese
Prop Stylist: Laura Ferguson
Photo Production Coordinator: Juliann Harvey
Photo Assistant: Kevin Hossler
Food Styling Assistant: Jill Sorensen
Glossary Illustrations: Alice Harth

A NOTE ON WEIGHTS AND MEASURES
All recipes include customary U.S. and metric
measurements. Metric conversions are based on a
standard developed for these books and have been
rounded off. Actual weights may vary.

The Williams-Sonoma Lifestyles Series
conceived and produced by Weldon Owen Inc.
814 Montgomery Street, San Francisco, CA 94133

In collaboration with Williams-Sonoma
3250 Van Ness Avenue, San Francisco, CA 94109

Separations by Colourscan Overseas Co. Pte. Ltd.
Printed in Singapore by Tien Wah Press (Pte.) Ltd.

A WELDON OWEN PRODUCTION
Copyright © 1998 Weldon Owen Inc.
All rights reserved, including the right of reproduc-
tion in whole or in part in any form.

First printed in 1998
10 9 8 7 6 5 4 3 2 1

Library of Congress
Cataloging-in-Publication Data

Goldstein, Joyce Esersky.
    Soup for Supper / general editor, Chuck
Williams; recipes, Joyce Goldstein; photography,
Richard Eskite.
        p. cm. — (Williams-Sonoma lifestyles)
    Includes index.
    ISBN 0-7835-4615-7
    1. Soups 1. Williams, Chuck II. Title.
III. Series.
TX757.G55 1998
641.8'13—dc21   98-9457
                                      CIP

A NOTE ON NUTRITIONAL ANALYSIS
Each recipe is analyzed for significant nutrients per
serving. Not included in the analysis are ingredients
that are optional or added to taste, or are suggested
as an alternative or substitution either in the recipe
or in the recipe introduction or accompanying tip.
In recipes that yield a range of servings, the analysis
is for the middle of that range.

Contents

Welcome

I can think of few foods more satisfying, both to make and to eat, than soup. A pot simmering on the back of the stove is a comforting sight in any kitchen, and when it's time to eat, soup soothes the soul with every spoonful.

One of my favorite ways to enjoy homemade soup is as a suppertime main dish. While it cooks, there's time to toss a salad, bake a quick bread, and make a simple dessert. It's easy to put an inviting meal on the table when soup is the featured course.

The great variety of soups makes it possible to serve one for nearly every occasion. Old-fashioned tomato soup is perfect for a casual family supper, while an elegant seafood bisque will dazzle special guests.

Whether your meal plans are simple or grand, this book contains all the recipes and information you will need to give soup a starring role. In addition to 30 soup recipes, there are 15 others for salads, sandwiches, and breads, and desserts to complement whatever soup you choose. A comprehensive introduction covers the basics of serving with style, making and storing stock, preparing garnishes and other embellishments, and planning menus.

All these features share a common goal: to help you enjoy the pleasures of making and serving soup for supper.

Chuck Williams

Serving Soup for Supper

Part of the beauty of making soup is that it requires only a few basic pieces of equipment. A heavy-bottomed pot conducts heat evenly and allows a soup to simmer unattended without fear of scorching. A food mill strains and purées a soup at the same time. A perforated skimmer helps remove the impurities from homemade stock. A ladle is the best tool for transferring the finished soup to serving bowls. A wooden spoon is ideal for stirring because it doesn't conduct heat.

Soups for Every Occasion

The occasions on which soups can be served vary as widely as the recipes in this book. There are soups that make a weekday family dinner special, such as Chicken, Tortilla, and Lime Soup (page 58), or can set the tone for an elegant evening of entertaining, such as Avocado Soup with Shrimp and Salsa (page 25). Heartier offerings, like Beef Barley Soup (page 46) or New England Clam Chowder (page 62), bring comfort on a chilly weekend. And still others, such as Wonton Soup (page 45), are worthy of a casual celebration.

Since preparing soup is often a leisurely affair, there's plenty of time to make the few additional dishes you need to round out the meal. Perhaps you'll want to make a batch of salsa to garnish a soup or toast croutons to add at the table (see pages 14–15). It takes only a few minutes to make a salad (pages 78–87), or some sandwiches or to bake a batch of biscuits (pages 88–97). And if you're in the mood for something sweet, prepare a simple dessert (pages 98–107). Then all you need to do is pour your favorite wine, beer, or other beverage.

When it comes to setting the table, there are many options for serving soup, including (far left) deep bowls, rimmed shallow soup plates, and mugs. Large spoons (left) with generously sized bowls ensure you'll enjoy every last mouthful. A tureen (below) lets you present soup at the table in classic style.

Presenting Soup in Style

Let the soup and the occasion suggest where you might serve it. The dining room or the kitchen table are the first, most obvious choices. But perhaps a wintry day will inspire you to ladle up a hearty soup beside the fireplace, or a hot summer's evening lead you to offer an ice-cold soup in the garden.

Wherever you decide to enjoy your soup meals, you'll want to have a few serving pieces on hand. For casual suppers, ladle soup directly from the pot. An attractive pot, perhaps a copper kettle or one made of enameled cast iron, can go directly on the table (just be sure to have trivets in place to protect the surface).

For classic soup service, consider a tureen that includes a lid to help keep soup hot. Any large, attractive, sturdy bowl will also do. Always rinse any serving vessel with hot tap water to warm it before filling it with a hot soup, again to guard against quick cooling.

To keep chilled soups cold, try nesting the serving bowl inside a larger bowl partially filled with crushed ice.

As for the individual serving bowls, you have two basic choices. Deep soup bowls are best for more casual meals. Broader, shallower soup plates, usually with wide rims, are particularly nice for showing off soups that include attractive pieces of ingredients. You can also ladle soup into large, sturdy mugs for informal meals or buffets.

Making Stock

Homemade stock provides soups with a flavorful foundation that no commercial product can rival; plus, making your own stock is one of the most satisfying of all kitchen tasks. The actual prep time is often less than 20 minutes, and in no more than a few hours (just 30 minutes for fish stock), you will have plenty of stock on hand for future soup meals.

If you decide to buy stock, choose a quality brand. Many specialty-food shops and food stores carry canned, concentrated, and frozen stocks. Look for canned stocks labeled "low sodium," for greater leeway in seasoning. Bottled clam juice makes a fine substitute for fish stock. Dilute it with water if you find the taste too strong.

SKIMMING THE SURFACE

1. As the water for stock slowly heats, it draws from the ingredients albuminous impurities that rise to the surface as a frothy scum. This should be skimmed away, or the stock will be cloudy and have a muddy flavor. Begin by heating in the water only the chicken parts or meat bones, sources of most of the scum.

ADDING THE AROMATICS

2. After the initial skimming is completed, add the aromatic vegetables and seasonings. Reskim any scum rising from the vegetables.

STRAINING THE STOCK

3. After the stock has simmered for the specified time, scoop out the larger solids with a slotted spoon. Dampen a double thickness of cheesecloth (muslin), which helps trap fat and particles, use it to line a fine-mesh sieve, and then pour the stock through it into a large bowl.

DISCARDING THE FAT

4. If you need to use the stock right away, blot up the liquid fat from its surface with a folded paper towel. If you have more time, refrigerate until well chilled, then use a slotted spoon to lift off and discard the solidified fat.

Chicken Stock

6 lb (3 kg) chicken parts such as
   necks, backs, wings, and thighs
2 yellow onions, coarsely chopped
2 small carrots, coarsely chopped
1 large celery stalk, chopped
green tops of 2 leeks, chopped
   (optional)
2 cloves garlic
2 or 3 fresh parsley sprigs
6–8 peppercorns
2 or 3 fresh thyme sprigs
2 small bay leaves

✲ Rinse the chicken parts, place in a stockpot, and add water to cover by 3 inches (7.5 cm). Bring to a boil, reduce the heat to low, and skim off any scum from the surface. Simmer, uncovered, for 1 hour, skimming as needed.

✲ Add all the remaining ingredients, cover partially, and simmer gently for about 4 hours. Remove from the heat.

✲ Scoop out and discard the solids, then pour through a fine-mesh sieve lined with damp cheesecloth (muslin) into 1 or more storage containers. Refrigerate, uncovered, until well chilled and the fat has solidified on top. Lift off and discard the fat. Use the stock at this point or cover and refrigerate for up to 5 days or freeze for up to 3 months.

MAKES ABOUT
4 QT (4 L)

STORING STOCK

The recipes here and on the previous page yield enough stock to form the base for several different batches of soup. Refrigerate any stock not used right away or store it in the freezer.

To refrigerate stock, transfer it to a container with a tight-fitting lid. Fish stock will keep for up to 2 days, beef stock for up to 4 days, chicken stock for up to 5 days, and vegetable stock for up to 1 week.

To freeze stock, line small, straight-sided freezer containers with heavy-duty lock-top plastic bags. Ladle in the stock in measured amounts, such as 1 or 2 cups (8 or 16 fl oz/250 or 500 ml), freeze, then pull the bags from the containers, seal airtight, and label them. All stocks will keep in the freezer for up to 3 months.

Beef Stock

6 lb (3 kg) meaty beef shanks, cracked
1 marrowbone, cracked
2 yellow onions, chopped
2 carrots, chopped
1 celery stalk, chopped
1 leek, chopped (optional)
2 cups (16 fl oz/500 ml) water
2 tomatoes, halved
6 cloves garlic
5 fresh parsley sprigs
2 small bay leaves
3 fresh thyme sprigs
8 peppercorns
2 whole cloves
mushroom stems (optional)

❋ Preheat an oven to 450°F (230°C). Place the shanks and marrowbone in a roasting pan. Roast, turning occasionally, until browned, about 1½ hours. Transfer to a stockpot, but do not clean the roasting pan. Add water to cover the bones by 4 inches (10 cm) and bring to a boil, skimming often. Reduce the heat to low and simmer, uncovered, for 1–2 hours, skimming occasionally.

❋ Meanwhile, brown the onions, carrots, celery, and leek (if using) in the roasting pan over medium-high heat until caramelized, 15–20 minutes. Add to the stockpot. Pour the water into the roasting pan and deglaze over medium-high heat, stirring to remove any browned bits from the pan bottom. Set aside.

❋ When the shanks have simmered for 1–2 hours, add the deglazed juices to the stockpot along with all the remaining ingredients. Cover partially and simmer gently for at least 4 hours or up to 8 hours.

❋ Remove from the heat. Scoop out and discard all the solids, then pour through a fine-mesh sieve lined with damp cheesecloth (muslin) into 1 or more storage containers. Refrigerate, uncovered, until well chilled and the fat has solidified on top. Lift off and discard the fat. Use the stock at this point or cover and refrigerate for up to 4 days or freeze for up to 3 months.

MAKES ABOUT 4 QT (4 L)

Fish Stock

2 tablespoons olive oil
4 lb (2 kg) fish frames from mild fish, including heads and tails but gills removed, rinsed under cold water
2 cups (16 fl oz/500 ml) dry white wine
2 or 3 yellow onions, coarsely chopped
3 celery stalks, coarsely chopped
2 lemon zest strips
3 fresh parsley sprigs
2 fresh thyme sprigs
5–8 peppercorns
3 whole coriander seeds
2 whole allspice
1 small bay leaf
1 walnut-sized piece fresh ginger, peeled (optional) and lightly crushed
6 cups (48 fl oz/1.5 l) water, or as needed

❀ In a stockpot over medium heat, warm the oil. Add the fish frames and sauté, stirring often, until they give off a little liquid, about 10 minutes. Add all the remaining ingredients including water as needed to immerse the bones. Bring to a boil, skim off any scum, reduce the heat to low, and simmer, uncovered, for 30 minutes, skimming often.

❀ Remove from the heat and strain through a fine-mesh sieve lined with damp cheesecloth (muslin). Use the stock at this point or transfer to a container. Refrigerate, uncovered, until cold, then cover and refrigerate for up to 2 days or freeze for up to 3 months.

MAKES ABOUT 8 CUPS
(64 FL OZ/2 L)

Vegetable Stock

5 carrots, cut into chunks
3 leeks, cut into chunks
3 celery stalks, cut into chunks
2 yellow onions, quartered
1 red (Spanish) onion, quartered
1 head garlic, halved
2 fresh thyme sprigs
1 bay leaf
5 peppercorns
4 qt (4 l) water

❀ Preheat an oven to 450°F (230°C).

❀ Place the carrots, leeks, celery, yellow and red onions, and garlic in a roasting pan. Roast, uncovered, stirring occasionally, until well browned, about 1 hour.

❀ Transfer the vegetables to a stockpot. Add the thyme sprigs, bay leaf, and peppercorns, and then pour in the water. Bring to a boil over high heat, cover, reduce the heat to low, and simmer for 1 hour.

❀ Remove from the heat. Strain through a fine-mesh sieve lined with damp cheesecloth (muslin). Use the stock at this point or transfer to 1 or more storage containers. Refrigerate, uncovered, until cold, then cover and refrigerate for up to 1 week or freeze for up to 3 months.

MAKES 3½–4 QT (3.5–4 L)

Roasting the ingredients for meat or vegetable stocks gives them a richly browned exterior that intensifies the flavor of the stock. Here, the aromatic ingredients for Vegetable Stock emerge from the oven deeply colored from the caramelization of their natural sugars.

Extras That Make a Difference

Enhancing Soups

Hearty main-course soups are often distinguished by special flourishes—additions, garnishes, or enrichments—that give them added texture and flavor. The photographs and captions shown here illustrate and explain techniques behind some of the most popular embellishments, from dumplings and stuffed pastas to croutons and salsas. You'll find other ideas throughout the book, or perhaps you have your own favorite ways to dress up soups. Among the easiest are scatterings of chopped fresh herbs such as dill for seafood soups or basil for vegetable-packed ones. Many soups also benefit from drizzling a stream of heavy cream or fragrant extra-virgin olive oil into each bowl at serving time.

Pastes made from starches like bread and nuts add both flavor and body. Here, a savory enrichment of almonds, bread, and garlic is pulverized in a mortar to make *picada*, which enhances Spanish Pumpkin and Bean Soup (page 22).

SHAPING MATZO BALLS

Dumpling mixtures such as that for matzo balls (page 53) must be chilled until firm enough to shape. Dampening your hands and a spoon makes it easier to form the dough neatly into spheres, ready to chill again before simmering.

FRYING TORTILLA STRIPS

Fried corn tortillas become a crisp, tasty garnish for Chicken, Tortilla, and Lime Soup (page 58). Heat oil to 375°F (190°C). Fry the strips in batches until crisp and golden. Remove with tongs and drain on paper towels.

ASSEMBLING WONTONS

Store-bought wrappers make it easy to stuff wontons for Wonton Soup (page 45). Moisten the edges with a cornstarch-water mixture. Spoon on the seasoned filling, then fold and press the edges to seal.

MIXING SALSA

Added at the table, a fresh avocado salsa spikes hot and cold soups alike, including Black Bean Soup (page 65). Combine and season the ingredients, chief among them tomato, chiles, and onion, just before serving.

FRYING CROUTONS

To make the crisp croutons that garnish Gazpacho (page 34), start with a coarse country loaf. In a frying pan, heat unsalted butter, olive oil, and a crushed garlic clove. Add bread cubes and sauté until golden brown.

Some soups show off at the table by being presented with a wide array of garnishes. Here, Cold Lithuanian Beet Borscht (page 28) is accompanied with chopped cucumber, green (spring) onion, hard-cooked eggs, potatoes, and sour cream.

Planning Menus

The recipes in this book were developed to complement one another. By choosing among them, it is possible to put together a satisfying supper for almost any occasion. The 10 menus here illustrate only a handful of the many possibilities. When planning your own meals, keep in mind the character of the featured soup. For example, filling ones that combine both vegetables and proteins go well with simple salads and light desserts. In contrast, when serving soups that feature a single ingredient, like Fresh Corn Soup or Hearty Split-Pea, you may want to offer both a sandwich and a salad, as well as dessert.

Autumn Picnic

Romaine, Gorgonzola,
and Walnut Salad
PAGE 87

Creamy Mushroom Soup
PAGE 71

Gougères
PAGE 89

Ginger Cookies
PAGE 99

Seafood Lover's Feast

Green Bean and New Potato
Salad with Salsa Verde
PAGE 83

Cioppino
PAGE 37

Lemon-Scented Ricotta
PAGE 102

Light Summer Meal

Fresh Corn Soup
PAGE 61

Cheese and Chile Quesadillas
PAGE 90

Tossed Green Salad

Amaretti-Stuffed
Baked Peaches
PAGE 105

Fall Fireside Supper

Celery, Mushroom,
and Endive Salad
PAGE 84

Rye Bread

Stuffed-Cabbage Soup
PAGE 49

Dried-Fruit Compote
PAGE 106

Mediterranean Summer

Tomato, Cucumber,
and Onion Salad with
Feta Vinaigrette
PAGE 80

Roasted Eggplant Soup
PAGE 75

Toasted Pita Bread

Mixed Fruit Gratin
PAGE 100

Elegant Dinner Party

Celery, Mushroom,
and Endive Salad
PAGE 84

Mussel Bisque with Saffron
PAGE 41

Baguette

Lemon-Scented Ricotta
PAGE 102

Thermos and Basket

Fresh Tomato Soup
PAGE 50

Mediterranean
Egg Salad Sandwich
PAGE 93

Ginger Cookies
PAGE 99

Casual Evening In

Grilled Fontina Sandwich
with Prosciutto and Pear
PAGE 97

Hearty Split-Pea Soup
PAGE 69

Fresh Fruit

Pan-Asian Lunch

Carrot, Apple, and
Red Cabbage Slaw with
Ginger Vinaigrette
PAGE 79

Chicken Coconut Soup
with Lemongrass
PAGE 21

Ginger Cookies
PAGE 99

Winter Repast

Romaine, Gorgonzola,
and Walnut Salad
PAGE 87

Roast Turkey Vegetable Soup
PAGE 19

Buttermilk Chive Biscuits
PAGE 94

Dried-Fruit Compote
PAGE 106

Roast Turkey Vegetable Soup with Rice

PREP TIME: 30 MINUTES, PLUS
9 HOURS FOR MAKING AND
CHILLING STOCK

COOKING TIME: 25 MINUTES

INGREDIENTS

TURKEY STOCK

carcass from roast turkey

3–3½ qt (3–3.5 l) water, or as needed

I large yellow onion, chopped

2 carrots, peeled and chopped

I celery stalk, chopped

4 fresh parsley sprigs

3 fresh thyme sprigs

I bay leaf

5 tablespoons (2½ fl oz/75 ml) olive oil

1½ cups (6 oz/185 g) chopped
   yellow onion

⅔ cup (3 oz/90 g) peeled and
   diced carrot

½ cup (2½ oz/75 g) diced celery

⅔ cup (4½ oz/140 g) long-grain
   white rice

2 cups (6 oz/185 g) sliced fresh
   mushrooms

2 cups (4 oz/125 g) broccoli florets

2 cups (12 oz/375 g) diced cooked
   turkey

2 teaspoons chopped fresh thyme

salt and ground pepper to taste

¼ cup (⅓ oz/10 g) chopped fresh
   flat-leaf (Italian) parsley (optional)

¼ cup (1 oz/30 g) grated Parmesan
   cheese (optional)

Next time you serve a roast turkey, use the leftovers to make this comforting soup. Cut off any meat that's clinging to the bones and wrap it so it doesn't dry out. Then use the carcass to make the stock.

SERVES 6–8

❀ To make the stock, with your hands, break the carcass into big pieces and place them in a large stockpot with water to cover. Bring to a boil, skimming off any foam that forms on the surface. Reduce the heat to low, cover, and simmer for about 1 hour, skimming as needed. Add the onion, carrots, celery, herb sprigs, and bay leaf. Cover partially and continue to simmer for about 1½ hours longer. Line a fine-mesh sieve with damp cheesecloth (muslin), pour the stock through the sieve into a large saucepan, and return to high heat. Bring to a boil, adjust the heat to maintain a gentle boil, and cook uncovered, skimming if needed, until reduced to about 8 cups (64 fl oz/2 l), about 1 hour. Remove from the heat and refrigerate, uncovered, until chilled, about 6 hours, then lift off and discard the fat solidified on top.

❀ In a large saucepan over medium heat, warm 2 tablespoons of the olive oil. Add the onion, carrot, and celery and sauté, stirring often, until the onion is tender and translucent, about 10 minutes. Add the rice and stock and bring to a boil. Reduce the heat to low and simmer until the rice is tender, about 15 minutes.

❀ Meanwhile, in a sauté pan over medium-high heat, warm the remaining 3 tablespoons oil. Add the mushrooms and sauté, stirring often, until tender, 8–10 minutes. Set aside. Bring a saucepan three-fourths full of lightly salted water to a boil, add the broccoli florets, and cook until tender but not falling apart, about 5 minutes. Drain, immerse in cold water to halt the cooking, drain again, and set aside.

❀ Add the turkey, mushrooms, broccoli, and thyme to the saucepan and continue to cook until all the ingredients are heated through, about 10 minutes. Season with salt and pepper.

❀ Ladle into warmed bowls and sprinkle with the parsley or Parmesan cheese, if using.

NUTRITIONAL ANALYSIS PER SERVING: Calories 296 (Kilojoules 1,243); Protein 20 g; Carbohydrates 23 g; Total Fat 14 g; Saturated Fat 3 g; Cholesterol 41 mg; Sodium 166 mg; Dietary Fiber 2 g

Chicken Coconut Soup with Lemongrass

PREP TIME: 15 MINUTES

COOKING TIME: 15 MINUTES

INGREDIENTS

4 cups (32 fl oz/1 l) Chicken Stock (page 11)

8 large slices peeled fresh galangal or 4 slices peeled fresh ginger

1 large lemongrass stalk, cut into 2-inch (5-cm) pieces, crushed

16 fresh kaffir lime leaves, torn in half, or grated zest of 1 large lime

2 cans (14 fl oz/430 ml each) coconut milk

¼ cup (2 fl oz/60 ml) lime or lemon juice

2–3 tablespoons Thai fish sauce

2 tablespoons light brown sugar

1 tablespoon red chile paste

1 lb (500 g) boneless, skinless chicken breasts, cut into bite-sized pieces

½ lb (250 g) fresh white mushrooms, brushed clean and thinly sliced

5 small fresh red or green chiles, sliced crosswise paper-thin

fresh cilantro (fresh coriander) leaves

SERVING TIP: To make this into a more substantial meal, add 1 cup (5 oz/155 g) cooked white rice to each bowl before ladling in the soup.

One of the most requested dishes in Thai restaurants is this soup, called *tom kha gai*. It is also easy to prepare at home, however, once you have the right ingredients on hand. While you may not be able to find kaffir lime leaves or galangal (a gingerlike rhizome) at your market, grated lime zest and fresh ginger work well in their place. Bottled fish sauce and canned coconut milk are now widely available, so this delicate and fragrant soup can grace your table often.

SERVES 4–6

❀ In a large saucepan, combine the stock, galangal or ginger, lemongrass, and lime leaves or lime zest. Place over medium heat and slowly bring to a boil. Boil for 1 minute.

❀ Reduce the heat to low, add the coconut milk, stir to combine, and bring to a simmer. Add the lime or lemon juice, fish sauce, brown sugar, and chile paste; mix well, and simmer for 5 minutes. Add the chicken pieces and simmer until tender, 4–5 minutes. Add the mushrooms and simmer until tender, about 1 minute longer.

❀ To serve, ladle into warmed bowls. Float the chile slices and cilantro leaves on top.

NUTRITIONAL ANALYSIS PER SERVING: Calories 500 (Kilojoules 2,100); Protein 29 g; Carbohydrates 19 g; Total Fat 37 g; Saturated Fat 31 g; Cholesterol 55 mg; Sodium 541 mg; Dietary Fiber 1 g

Spanish Pumpkin and Bean Soup

PREP TIME: 40 MINUTES,
PLUS 8 HOURS FOR
SOAKING BEANS

COOKING TIME: 1¼ HOURS

INGREDIENTS

1 cup (7 oz/220 g) dried chickpeas (garbanzo beans)

1 cup (7 oz/220 g) small dried white beans such as Great Northern

2 qt (2 l) plus 3 cups (24 fl oz/750 ml) water

½ cup (4 fl oz/125 ml) olive oil

1 large yellow onion, chopped

¼ cup (1½ oz/45 g) diced ham

1 tablespoon sweet paprika

2 tomatoes, peeled, seeded, and diced

pinch of saffron, steeped in ¼ cup (2 fl oz/60 ml) hot Chicken Stock (page 11) or water

12 almonds

1 slice bread, cut in half

2 cloves garlic

2 tablespoons sherry vinegar

1½ cups (8 oz/250 g) peeled and coarsely chopped pumpkin or butternut squash

3 pears, halved, cored, peeled, and cut into chunks

½ lb (250 g) green beans, trimmed and cut into 2-inch (5-cm) lengths

salt and ground pepper to taste

This chunky soup is made even more interesting with the addition of diced pears and a classic Catalan *picada* thickener of garlic, almonds, and bread. In Morocco, lentils might be used instead of chickpeas or white beans, and sometimes rice or braised greens are added to the mix.

SERVES 6–8

❋ Pick over the chickpeas and white beans, discarding any misshapen beans or stones. Rinse the chickpeas and beans and drain. Place in a bowl, add plenty of water to cover, and let soak overnight. The next day, drain them. In a saucepan over high heat, bring the 2 quarts (2 l) plus 3 cups (24 fl oz/750 ml) water to a boil. When the water is boiling, add the chickpeas and beans. When the water returns to a boil, reduce the heat to low and simmer until tender, about 1 hour.

❋ Meanwhile, in a sauté pan over medium heat, warm 2 tablespoons of the olive oil. Add the onion and sauté, stirring occasionally, until tender and translucent, about 10 minutes. Stir in the ham and paprika, mixing well, and then mix in the tomatoes. Cook for 10 minutes to blend the flavors. Add the saffron and liquid to the pan, mix well, and set aside.

❋ Pour the remaining 6 tablespoons (3 fl oz/90 ml) olive oil into another sauté pan and place over medium heat. Add the almonds, bread, and garlic, and cook, stirring occasionally, until golden, about 5 minutes. Using a slotted spoon, transfer the almonds, bread, and garlic to a mortar or a small food processor. Grind with a pestle or process to a paste. Add the vinegar to the paste, mixing well. Set aside.

❋ After the beans have cooked for 1 hour, add the pumpkin or butternut squash and the pears and simmer for 10 minutes. Finally, stir in the tomato-onion mixture, the green beans, and the bread mixture and simmer until the green beans and squash are tender and the flavors are blended, 10–15 minutes. Season with salt and pepper.

❋ Ladle into warmed bowls and serve immediately.

NUTRITIONAL ANALYSIS PER SERVING: Calories 452 (Kilojoules 1,898); Protein 15 g; Carbohydrates 58 g; Total Fat 20 g; Saturated Fat 3 g; Cholesterol 4 mg; Sodium 123 mg; Dietary Fiber 17 g

Avocado Soup with Shrimp and Salsa

PREP TIME: 20 MINUTES, PLUS
1 HOUR FOR CHILLING

INGREDIENTS

3 large avocados, halved, pitted,
   peeled, and diced

3 cups (24 fl oz/750 ml) Chicken
   Stock (page 11), or as needed

1–1½ cups (8–12 fl oz/250–375 ml)
   heavy (double) cream

2 tablespoons lemon juice, or to taste

salt and ground pepper to taste

TOMATO SALSA

1½ cups (10½ oz/330 g) finely
   chopped tomato

⅓ cup (2 oz/60 g) finely minced red
   onion

2 or 3 jalapeño chiles, finely minced,
   with or without seeds to taste

2 cloves garlic, finely minced

3 tablespoons lemon or lime juice,
   or to taste

¼ cup (⅓ oz/10 g) chopped fresh
   cilantro (fresh coriander)

¼ cup (2 fl oz/60 ml) olive oil

salt and ground pepper to taste

12–16 cooked shrimp (prawns),
   peeled and diced

Usually served chilled, this Latin American soup is also delicious at room temperature. The zesty tomato salsa provides a lively contrast to the rich and creamy flavor of the avocado. Fresh cooked crabmeat can be substituted for the shrimp, if you like.

SERVES 6–8

✣ Working in 2 or 3 batches, combine the avocados, stock, and cream in a blender. Purée until smooth. Adjust the amount of cream used as needed to arrive at a good soup consistency. Transfer to a bowl. Season with lemon juice, salt, and pepper. Cover and refrigerate until cold but not overly chilled, about 1 hour.

✣ Meanwhile, make the tomato salsa: In a bowl, combine the tomato, onion, chiles, garlic, lemon or lime juice, cilantro, olive oil, salt, and pepper. Stir well, taste, and adjust the seasonings.

✣ To serve, remove the soup from the refrigerator and taste and adjust the seasonings. Ladle the soup into chilled individual bowls. Top each serving with some of the diced shrimp and a generous dollop of the salsa.

NUTRITIONAL ANALYSIS PER SERVING: Calories 436 (Kilojoules 1,831); Protein 11 g; Carbohydrates 13 g; Total Fat 40 g; Saturated Fat 14 g; Cholesterol 121 mg; Sodium 107 mg; Dietary Fiber 3 g

PREP TIP: Make a green salsa by substituting tomatillos for the tomatoes in the salsa recipe.

Meatball Soup

PREP TIME: 45 MINUTES

COOKING TIME: 45 MINUTES

INGREDIENTS

MEATBALLS

½ lb (250 g) ground (minced) beef, veal, or lamb

½ cup (1 oz/30 g) fresh bread crumbs

¼ cup (1½ oz/45 g) grated yellow onion

1 egg

¼ cup (⅓ oz/10 g) chopped fresh flat-leaf (Italian) parsley

1 clove garlic, finely minced (optional)

½ teaspoon each ground cinnamon and ground cumin (optional)

salt and ground pepper to taste

1 teaspoon vegetable oil

SOUP BASE

2 tablespoons olive oil

1½ cups (6 oz/185 g) chopped yellow onion

8 cups (64 fl oz/2 l) Beef Stock (page 12)

2–3 cups (16–24 fl oz/500–750 ml) canned tomato purée

3 cups (1¼ lb/625 g) cooked chopped greens such as escarole or chicory (optional)

2 cups (10 oz/315 g) cooked white rice or short pasta (optional)

salt and ground pepper to taste

¼ cup (⅓ oz/10 g) chopped fresh flat-leaf (Italian) parsley (optional)

Instead of poaching the meatballs directly in the soup, you can sauté them first in a little olive oil until golden and then add them to the hot broth. Sautéing them first gives them a firmer texture and darker color. Cooked rice, noodles, or braised greens can be added for a more filling meal.

SERVES 6

❊ To make the meatballs, in a bowl, combine the meat, bread crumbs, onion, egg, parsley, and, if using, the garlic, cinnamon, and cumin. Mix well, then season with salt and pepper. In a small frying pan, heat the 1 teaspoon of oil over medium-high heat. When hot, fry a tiny nugget of the mixture until cooked through, taste, and adjust the seasonings if needed. Line a large baking sheet with parchment (baking) paper. Form the meat mixture into tiny meatballs, each about the size of a marble and place on the prepared baking sheet in a single layer. Cover and refrigerate until ready to cook.

❊ To make the soup base, in a large saucepan over medium heat, warm the 2 tablespoons olive oil. Add the onion and sauté, stirring occasionally, until tender and translucent, about 10 minutes. Raise the heat to high and add the stock and tomato purée and bring to a boil. Reduce the heat to low and simmer for 10 minutes.

❊ Gently slip the meatballs into the soup base and simmer over low heat until the meatballs are cooked through and tender, about 20 minutes. Add the cooked greens and the rice or pasta, if using, and simmer until heated through, about 5 minutes longer. Taste and adjust the seasonings.

❊ Ladle into warmed bowls and garnish with the parsley, if desired. Serve immediately.

NUTRITIONAL ANALYSIS PER SERVING: Calories 281 (Kilojoules 1,180); Protein 16 g; Carbohydrates 20 g; Total Fat 16 g; Saturated Fat 5 g; Cholesterol 68 mg; Sodium 575 mg; Dietary Fiber 4 g

Cold Lithuanian Beet Borscht

PREP TIME: 40 MINUTES

COOKING TIME: 50 MINUTES,
    PLUS 6 HOURS FOR
    CHILLING

INGREDIENTS

6–8 large beets, 3½–4 lb (1.75–2 kg)
    total weight

about ½ cup (4 fl oz/125 ml) red wine

2 tablespoons unsalted butter

2 red (Spanish) onions, diced

1–1½ cups (8–12 fl oz/250–375 ml)
    Chicken Stock (page 11)

3–4 cups (24–32 fl oz/750 ml–1 l)
    buttermilk

salt and ground pepper to taste

2 tablespoons raspberry or other
    fruit-flavored vinegar or lemon
    juice, or to taste

pinch of sugar (optional)

6 small or medium boiling potatoes,
    peeled and coarsely diced

1½ cups (7½ oz/235 g) peeled,
    seeded, and diced cucumber

½ cup (1½ oz/45 g) minced green
    (spring) onion

3 hard-cooked eggs, peeled and
    coarsely chopped

6 tablespoons (3 fl oz/90 ml) sour
    cream or plain yogurt (optional)

Unlike a Russian borscht, which is clear, this Lithuanian version calls for buttermilk, which adds a creamy tartness. It is a spectacularly vibrant-looking soup. It makes a satisfying summer meal served with some good dark rye bread.

SERVES 6

❋ Peel 1 beet and grate it into a bowl. Pour in the red wine; it should cover the beet. Set aside. Trim the stems from the remaining beets, leaving about ½ inch (12 mm) intact; do not peel. Place in a large saucepan, add water to cover, and bring to a boil. Reduce the heat to low, cover, and simmer until tender when pierced, 45–50 minutes. Drain, immerse in cold water to cool slightly, peel, then cut off the stems and root ends. Finely dice 1 cooked beet; set aside. Set the remaining beets aside separately.

❋ In a small saucepan over medium heat, melt the butter. Add the onions and sauté until tender and translucent, about 10 minutes. Add stock to cover, raise the heat to high, and bring to a boil. Reduce the heat to low and simmer, uncovered, until the onions are very soft, about 10 minutes. Remove from the heat.

❋ Slice the whole cooked beets and place in a blender. Add the cooked onions and their liquids and the grated beet and red wine and purée until smooth. Transfer to a bowl and add the buttermilk, using as much of it as is needed to balance the sweet and tart flavors of the soup. Season with salt and pepper. Add the vinegar or lemon juice and the sugar, if using. The balance of sweet and sour depends upon the taste of the cook, so add slowly and taste and adjust as you like. Stir in the reserved diced beet, cover, and refrigerate until well chilled, about 6 hours.

❋ About 15 minutes before serving, place the potatoes in a saucepan with lightly salted water to cover. Bring to a boil, reduce the heat to medium, and simmer, uncovered, until just tender, 5–7 minutes. Drain well and keep hot.

❋ To serve, ladle the soup into bowls. Garnish with the cucumber, green onion, hard-cooked eggs, and the hot potatoes. If desired, top each serving with a dollop of sour cream or yogurt or pass the bowl at the table.

NUTRITIONAL ANALYSIS PER SERVING: Calories 339 (Kilojoules 1,424); Protein 15 g; Carbohydrates 51 g; Total Fat 8 g; Saturated Fat 4 g; Cholesterol 123 mg; Sodium 356 mg; Dietary Fiber 5 g

Italian Bean and Pasta Soup

PREP TIME: 20 MINUTES,
    PLUS 1 HOUR FOR SOAKING
    BEANS

COOKING TIME: 1¼ HOURS

INGREDIENTS

2 cups (14 oz/440 g) dried cranberry (borlotti), cannellini, or other small white beans

3 tablespoons olive oil

½ cup (3 oz/90 g) chopped pancetta

1 yellow onion, chopped

2 carrots, peeled and chopped

2 celery stalks, chopped

4 large cloves garlic, minced

8 cups (64 fl oz/2 l) water or Chicken Stock (page 11), or as needed

1½ cups (9 oz/280 g) diced canned plum (Roma) tomatoes

2 teaspoons salt, plus salt to taste

ground pepper to taste

½ lb (250 g) small dried pasta such as shells or ditalini

extra-virgin olive oil for serving

grated Parmesan cheese for serving

COOKING TIP: Stir the soup often if reheating it, especially if you have puréed any of the beans, to prevent sticking and burning.

When the weather is cool and you feel like staying indoors, it's time to make *pasta e fagioli,* a favorite Italian meal in a bowl. It can be brothy or quite thick, depending upon personal taste. Cooking the pasta separately from the soup helps the pasta maintain its texture. If you have made the soup in advance, add the cooked pasta when reheating it, as the pasta can become mushy if it stands too long in the soup.

SERVES 6

❋ Pick over the beans and discard any misshapen beans or stones. Rinse the beans, drain, and place in a saucepan. Add water to cover and bring to a boil over high heat. Boil for 2 minutes, then remove from the heat, cover, and let stand for 1 hour. Drain.

❋ In a saucepan over medium heat, warm the olive oil. Add the pancetta and sauté, stirring often, until softened, about 5 minutes. Add the onion, carrots, celery, and garlic and sauté, stirring often, until softened, about 8 minutes longer. Add the water or stock, beans, tomatoes, and 2 teaspoons salt and bring to a boil. Cover, reduce the heat to low, and simmer until the beans are very tender, about 1 hour.

❋ To give the soup more body, remove 2 large spoonfuls of beans and vegetables and purée in a blender or food processor, then return the purée to the pan. Season with salt and pepper and reheat gently.

❋ When the soup is almost ready, bring a large saucepan three-fourths full of salted water to a boil. Add the pasta, stir well, and cook until barely al dente, about 8 minutes or according to package directions. Drain and add to the soup. Simmer for an additional 5 minutes.

❋ To serve, ladle into warmed bowls. Top each serving with a swirl of extra-virgin olive oil, some grated Parmesan cheese, and a liberal grinding of pepper.

NUTRITIONAL ANALYSIS PER SERVING: Calories 656 (Kilojoules 2,755); Protein 25 g; Carbohydrates 78 g; Total Fat 29 g; Saturated Fat 6 g; Cholesterol 13 mg; Sodium 1140 mg; Dietary Fiber 10 g

Roasted Butternut Squash Soup

PREP TIME: 30 MINUTES, PLUS
1¼ HOURS FOR BAKING
SQUASHES

COOKING TIME: 20 MINUTES

INGREDIENTS

2 large butternut squashes, 1½–2 lb
(750 g–1 kg) each

⅓ cup (2 oz/60 g) hazelnuts (filberts)

6 tablespoons (3 oz/90 g) unsalted
butter

2 yellow onions, chopped

8 fresh sage leaves, shredded

6 cups (48 fl oz/1.5 l) Chicken Stock
(page 11) or Vegetable Stock
(page 13)

salt and ground pepper to taste

ground nutmeg to taste, if needed

pinch of sugar, if needed

SERVING TIP: For an elegant garnish,
whip about ¼ cup (6 fl oz/180 ml)
heavy (double) cream until stiff, season it with chopped fresh sage or
Marsala wine and ground nutmeg,
and place a little dollop on each bowl
just before serving.

Roasting the squash makes it easier to peel and seed, and deepens
the flavor of its flesh, making a richer, more flavorful soup.

SERVES 6

❋ Preheat an oven to 400°F (200°C).

❋ Prick each squash with the tip of a knife so it won't explode when it
bakes. Place the whole squashes on a baking sheet and roast until they
feel somewhat soft to the touch and a knife penetrates the skin easily,
about 1 hour. Remove from the oven and, when cool enough to handle,
cut in half lengthwise and remove and discard the seeds and fibers.
Scoop out the pulp into a bowl and set aside.

❋ While the squashes are cooling, reduce the oven temperature to 350°F
(180°C). Spread the hazelnuts on a baking sheet and toast until fragrant
and the skins have loosened, about 10 minutes. Remove from the oven
and, while still warm, place the nuts in a kitchen towel. Rub the towel
vigorously to remove the skins; do not worry if small bits of skin
remain. Chop and set aside.

❋ In a saucepan over low heat, melt the butter. Add the onions and half
of the sage and cook, stirring occasionally, until the onions are tender
and translucent, 8–10 minutes. Add the stock and squash pulp, raise the
heat to high, and bring to a boil. Reduce the heat to low and simmer for
a few minutes to combine the flavors. Remove from the heat.

❋ Working in batches, purée the soup in a blender or food processor.
Return to a clean saucepan. Alternatively, pass through a food mill
placed over the pan. Reheat gently over medium-low heat. Season with
salt and pepper. If the squash is starchy rather than sweet, a little nutmeg will help. If the nutmeg doesn't give the proper flavor balance, add
a pinch of sugar.

❋ Ladle into warmed bowls and garnish with the hazelnuts and the
remaining sage. Serve at once.

NUTRITIONAL ANALYSIS PER SERVING: Calories 312 (Kilojoules 1,310); Protein 7 g;
Carbohydrates 34 g; Total Fat 19 g; Saturated Fat 8 g; Cholesterol 34 mg; Sodium 106 mg;
Dietary Fiber 6 g

Gazpacho

PREP TIME: 30 MINUTES, PLUS
2 HOURS FOR CHILLING

INGREDIENTS

ice water, as needed

6–8 large beefsteak or other full-flavored tomatoes

1 small sweet yellow or red (Spanish) onion, chopped

4 cloves garlic

6 tablespoons (3 fl oz/90 ml) red wine vinegar, or to taste

2 regular or 1 English (hothouse) cucumber, halved, peeled, seeded, and diced

½ cup (4 fl oz/125 ml) extra-virgin olive oil, plus 2 tablespoons for frying croutons

salt and ground pepper to taste

3 or 4 thick (1-inch/2.5-cm) slices French or Italian bread, crusts removed and cut into 1-inch (2.5-cm) cubes

1 small green bell pepper (capsicum), seeded and finely diced

¼ cup (1¼ oz/37 g) finely minced red (Spanish) onion

SERVING TIP: For a more lavish gazpacho, add cooked and peeled shrimp (prawns) or chunks of lobster meat.

When the weather is hot and the tomato season is at its peak, make a huge batch of this soup. Bread is traditionally incorporated into the soup base (*gazpacho* means "soaked bread" in Arabic). Here, it is added later, in the form of garlic croutons, preferably warm, for a wonderful contrast of temperatures and textures.

SERVES 6–8

✤ Bring a large saucepan three-fourths full of water to a boil. Have ready a large bowl of ice water. Meanwhile, cut a shallow cross in the blossom end of each tomato, and then remove the core. Carefully slip the tomatoes into the boiling water for 30 seconds, then, using a slotted spoon, transfer to the ice water to cool. Remove from the water and peel immediately. Cut the tomatoes in half crosswise and squeeze out the seeds. In a blender or food processor, purée 3 of the tomatoes until liquefied and transfer to a large bowl. Reserve the remaining tomatoes.

✤ Put the onion in the blender or food processor. Chop 3 of the garlic cloves and add them as well. Purée, adding a bit of the vinegar if needed for a smooth consistency. Add to the bowl holding the tomato purée. Add the cucumbers with a little of the vinegar to the blender or processor and pulse until they are coarsely chopped. Add to the bowl as well. Chop the remaining tomatoes coarsely in the blender or processor. Add to the bowl. Whisk in the ½ cup (4 fl oz/125 ml) olive oil and the remaining vinegar, and season with salt and pepper. Serve now, or cover and refrigerate until well chilled, about 2 hours.

✤ Just before serving the soup, in a large frying pan over medium heat, warm the 2 tablespoons olive oil. Crush the remaining garlic clove, add to the pan, and cook for a minute or two to release its fragrance. Add the bread cubes and stir and toss until golden brown, about 5 minutes. Transfer to paper towels to drain; keep warm.

✤ Taste the soup and adjust the seasonings with salt. Ladle into chilled bowls and garnish each serving with the diced bell pepper and the minced onion. Float the croutons on top and serve.

NUTRITIONAL ANALYSIS PER SERVING: Calories 272 (Kilojoules 1,142); Protein 4 g; Carbohydrates 21 g; Total Fat 21 g; Saturated Fat 3 g; Cholesterol 0 mg; Sodium 99 mg; Dietary Fiber 4 g

Cioppino

PREP TIME: 45 MINUTES

COOKING TIME: 30 MINUTES

INGREDIENTS

½ cup (4 fl oz/125 ml) olive oil

3 cups (12 oz/375 g) chopped
   yellow onion

1 cup (4 oz/125 g) chopped celery

3 tablespoons minced garlic

2 small bay leaves

2 fresh thyme sprigs

2 teaspoons ground fennel seeds

1–2 teaspoons red pepper flakes

5 cups (40 fl oz/1.25 l) Fish Stock
   (page 13)

3 cups (18 oz/560 g) chopped canned
   plum (Roma) tomatoes, with their
   juices

1½ cups (12 fl oz/375 ml) dry red
   wine

½ cup (4 fl oz/125 ml) thick tomato
   purée

salt and ground black pepper to taste

18 clams, well scrubbed

1 crab or lobster, cooked, cracked,
   and sectioned into 2–3-inch
   (5–7.5-cm) pieces

18 mussels, well scrubbed and
   debearded

18 shrimp (prawns), peeled and
   deveined

18 sea scallops, tough muscles
   removed

¼ cup (⅓ oz/10 g) chopped fresh
   flat-leaf (Italian) parsley or basil

The origin of this famous San Francisco specialty is open to speculation. Most locals believe it is related to the Italian *cacciucco*, a fish stew of Livorno, and to the fish stews of the Friuli region, which are made with red wine. Serve with grilled coarse country bread rubbed with garlic.

SERVES 6

❀ In a large saucepan over medium heat, warm the olive oil. Add the onion and sauté, stirring occasionally, until translucent, about 5 minutes. Add the celery, garlic, bay leaves, thyme, fennel seeds, and red pepper flakes and cook until the celery is soft, about 5 minutes longer. Add the fish stock, tomatoes, wine, and tomato purée and simmer for about 10 minutes to blend the flavors. Season with salt and pepper.

❀ Add the clams to the pan along with the lobster or crab. Cover and simmer briskly until the clams start to open, about 5 minutes. Add the mussels, shrimp, and scallops and continue to cook until the mussels open, the shrimp turn pink, and the scallops are opaque throughout, 3–5 minutes.

❀ Ladle into warmed bowls and sprinkle with the parsley or basil. Serve immediately.

NUTRITIONAL ANALYSIS PER SERVING: Calories 480 (Kilojoules 2,016); Protein 42 g; Carbohydrates 19 g; Total Fat 24 g; Saturated Fat 3 g; Cholesterol 165 mg; Sodium 870 mg; Dietary Fiber 3 g

Caldo Verde

PREP TIME: 25 MINUTES

COOKING TIME: 30 MINUTES

INGREDIENTS

½ lb (250 g) chorizo, linguiça, or kielbasa sausages

¾ lb (375 g) kale or collard greens

¼ cup (2 fl oz/60 ml) olive oil

2 large yellow onions, chopped

3 or 4 potatoes, 1–1¼ lb (500–625 g) total weight, peeled and thinly sliced

3 or 4 cloves garlic, finely minced

6–7 cups (48–56 fl oz/1.5–1.75 l) water or Chicken Stock (page 11)

2 teaspoons salt, plus salt to taste

ground pepper to taste

extra-virgin olive oil for serving

COOKING TIP: You don't have to mash the potatoes; you may leave them in soft slices instead. The mashing, however, adds body to the soup.

The dark green cabbage traditionally used in this Portuguese "green" soup is not widely available beyond Portugal's borders, but kale or collard greens make a good substitute. A crusty corn bread called *broa* often accompanies the soup, although a good American corn bread is also nice for sopping up any bits remaining in the bowl. Don't forget the final flourish of olive oil. It will perfume the dish.

SERVES 6

❀ Bring a saucepan three-fourths full of water to a boil. Prick the sausages with a fork and add to the boiling water. Boil for about 5 minutes. Using tongs, transfer the sausages to a cutting board and, when cool enough to handle, slice them. (You may discard the sausage-flavored water or reserve it for making the soup.)

❀ Rinse and drain the greens, then remove any tough stems. Working in batches, stack the leaves, roll up the stack like a cigar, and cut crosswise into very, very thin strips. Set aside.

❀ In a large saucepan over medium heat, warm the olive oil. Add the onions and sauté, stirring occasionally, until tender and translucent, about 10 minutes. Raise the heat to medium-high, add the potatoes and garlic, and sauté, stirring often, until slightly softened, about 5 minutes. Add the water or stock and 2 teaspoons salt, cover, and simmer over low heat until the potatoes are very soft, about 20 minutes.

❀ Scoop out about 2 cups (10 oz/315 g) of the potatoes and mash well with a potato masher or fork. Return them to the pan, add the sliced sausage, and simmer until the sausage is cooked through, about 5 minutes longer. Add the greens, stir well, and simmer uncovered, stirring occasionally, for 3–5 minutes. Do not overcook; the greens should be bright green and slightly crunchy. Season with salt and pepper.

❀ To serve, ladle into warmed bowls and drizzle each bowl evenly with extra-virgin olive oil.

NUTRITIONAL ANALYSIS PER SERVING: Calories 422 (Kilojoules 1,772); Protein 13 g; Carbohydrates 25 g; Total Fat 31 g; Saturated Fat 8 g; Cholesterol 33 mg; Sodium 1275 mg; Dietary Fiber 6 g

Mussel Bisque with Saffron

PREP TIME: 40 MINUTES

COOKING TIME: 40 MINUTES

INGREDIENTS

5 lb (2.5 kg) mussels, well scrubbed

2 cups (16 fl oz/500 ml) dry white wine

about 4 cups (32 fl oz/1 l) water or Fish Stock (page 13)

¼ cup (2 oz/60 g) unsalted butter

1 cup (4 oz/125 g) chopped leek or yellow onion

½ cup (2 oz/60 g) chopped fennel (optional)

1 cup (6 oz/185 g) peeled, seeded, and chopped tomatoes (fresh or canned)

2 cups (10 oz/315 g) peeled and diced red potato

1 teaspoon saffron threads, steeped in ¼ cup (2 fl oz/60 ml) dry sherry

1 orange zest strip, 3 inches (7.5 cm) long

1½ cups (12 fl oz/375 ml) heavy (double) cream, heated

salt and ground pepper to taste

3 tablespoons chopped fresh flat-leaf (Italian) parsley or chervil

PREP TIP: There is no need to debeard the mussels before cooking them. You'll be able to remove the beards more easily once the shells have opened. Just be sure to scrub them well before cooking.

Although mussel bisque tastes complex, it is easy to prepare and is ideal for a special dinner. While it is festive and rich, it will not break the bank, as mussels are among the most reasonably priced shellfish at the market.

SERVES 6

❀ Discard any mussels that do not close to the touch. In a large, wide pan over high heat, combine the mussels and wine. Cover and cook, shaking the pan from time to time, until the mussels open, about 5 minutes. Remove from the heat and, when the mussels are cool enough to handle, discard any that did not open. Remove the remainder from their shells, picking off and discarding the beards and the shells. Pour the liquid through a sieve lined with damp cheesecloth (muslin) placed over a large bowl. Add water or fish stock as needed to measure about 6 cups (48 fl oz/1.5 l). Cover the cooked mussels with about 1 cup (8 fl oz/250 ml) of the cooking liquid and refrigerate.

❀ In a saucepan over medium heat, melt the butter. Add the leek or onion and the fennel, if using, and sauté, stirring occasionally, until softened, 8–10 minutes. Add the tomatoes, potato, saffron and sherry, orange zest, and the remaining 5 cups (40 fl oz/1.25 l) cooking liquid. Raise the heat to high and bring to a boil. Reduce the heat to low and simmer until the potato is soft, about 20 minutes.

❀ Select 18–24 perfect mussels for garnish and add the rest to the soup, along with the liquid in the bowl. Working in batches, purée the soup in a blender. Strain through a fine-mesh sieve placed over a heavy-bottomed saucepan. Add the cream and reheat very gently over very low heat, about 5 minutes. Season with salt and pepper.

❀ Ladle into warmed bowls. Garnish with the reserved whole mussels and the parsley or chervil and serve immediately.

NUTRITIONAL ANALYSIS PER SERVING: Calories 426 (Kilojoules 1,789); Protein 16 g; Carbohydrates 19 g; Total Fat 32 g; Saturated Fat 19 g; Cholesterol 133 mg; Sodium 352 mg; Dietary Fiber 1 g

Indian Red Lentil Soup

PREP TIME: 15 MINUTES

COOKING TIME: 45 MINUTES

INGREDIENTS

1½ cups (10½ oz/530 g) red lentils

3 tablespoons unsalted butter

1 large yellow onion, chopped

2 tablespoons ground coriander

2 teaspoons ground cumin

2 teaspoons peeled and grated fresh
    ginger

½ teaspoon ground turmeric

pinch of cayenne pepper

6 cups (48 fl oz/1.5 l) water,
    Vegetable Stock *(page 13)*, or
    Chicken Stock *(page 11)*

1½ cups (9 oz/280 g) peeled, seeded,
    and diced tomatoes (fresh or
    canned)

2 tablespoons lemon juice, or
    to taste

salt and ground black pepper
    to taste

3 tablespoons chopped fresh mint
    or cilantro (fresh coriander)

While lentil soup is usually comfort food, this variation makes it a bit exotic, too. The fragrant Indian spices lighten and brighten the simple, homey flavor of the soup. Red lentils have a tendency to break down into a coarse purée as they cook, so if you prefer some texture, omit the blender or food processor step.

SERVES 6

❋ Pick over the red lentils and discard any misshapen lentils or stones. Rinse the lentils and drain.

❋ In a saucepan over medium heat, melt the butter. Add the onion and sauté, stirring occasionally, until tender and translucent, 8–10 minutes. Add the coriander, cumin, ginger, turmeric, and cayenne and stir to mix well. Reduce the heat to low and cook, stirring occasionally, to release the flavors of the spices, 2–3 minutes. Add the lentils and then gradually add the water or stock, stirring constantly. Bring to a boil over high heat, reduce the heat to low, cover partially, and simmer until the lentils are very soft, 30–45 minutes.

❋ Remove from the heat and let cool slightly. Working in batches, purée the soup in a blender or food processor. Return the soup to a clean saucepan and place over medium heat. Stir in the tomatoes and lemon juice and cook until heated through. Season with salt and black pepper.

❋ To serve, ladle into warmed bowls and sprinkle with the mint or cilantro.

NUTRITIONAL ANALYSIS PER SERVING: Calories 303 (Kilojoules 1,273); Protein 20 g; Carbohydrates 44 g; Total Fat 7 g; Saturated Fat 4 g; Cholesterol 16 mg; Sodium 16 mg; Dietary Fiber 9 g

Wonton Soup

PREP TIME: 1 HOUR

COOKING TIME: 15 MINUTES

INGREDIENTS

WONTONS

½ lb (250 g) ground (minced) pork

¼ lb (125 g) peeled shrimp (prawns), chopped

¼ cup (1½ oz/45 g) finely minced water chestnuts

¼ cup (1 oz/30 g) finely minced green (spring) onions

1 egg

2 tablespoons light soy sauce

1 tablespoon dry sherry

2 teaspoons Asian sesame oil

1 teaspoon ginger juice *(see note)*

salt to taste, if needed

1 package (1 lb/500 g) wonton wrappers

2 teaspoons cornstarch (cornflour) dissolved in 2 tablespoons water

8 cups (64 fl oz/2 l) Chicken Stock *(page 11)* or low-sodium chicken broth simmered with 3–4 slices peeled fresh ginger for 10–15 minutes

1 large bunch spinach, tough stems removed and leaves cut into wide strips

MAKE-AHEAD TIP: The wontons can be made in advance and refrigerated for up to 1 day or frozen for up to 1 month.

All the world loves stuffed pasta served in a rich broth, whether it's tortellini, kreplach, or wontons. It is easy to find wonton wrappers in many food stores, so why not dazzle your family and friends with this delectable soup? To make ginger juice, grate ginger to a fine paste, place in a small, fine-mesh sieve, and press with the back of a spoon to extract the juice.

SERVES 6

❀ To make the wontons, in a medium bowl, combine the pork, shrimp, water chestnuts, and green onions. In a small bowl, whisk together the egg, soy sauce, sherry, sesame oil, and ginger juice. Stir the egg mixture into the pork mixture, mixing well. Bring a saucepan three-fourths full of water to a boil, add a small ball of the pork mixture to the water, and poach until cooked through, 2–3 minutes. Drain, taste, and adjust the seasonings with soy, ginger, or a little salt.

❀ To assemble the wontons, lay out 10 wonton wrappers on a work surface. Place a teaspoon or so of the mixture on the center of each wrapper. Dip your finger in the cornstarch mixture and spread along two edges of each wrapper. Fold each in half on the diagonal to form a triangle and press the seams to seal securely. Place on a baking sheet. Repeat until all the stuffing is used; you should have about 48 wontons. Wrap any leftover wrappers airtight and store in the refrigerator for up to 1 week. Refrigerate the wontons until needed.

❀ In a large saucepan, bring the stock to a boil over high heat, then reduce the heat to low to maintain a gentle simmer. At the same time, bring a large saucepan half-full of water to a boil. Carefully drop the wontons into the boiling water. When the water returns to a boil, add 1½ cups (12 fl oz/375 ml) cold water. When the water returns to a boil, add 1 more cup (8 fl oz/250 ml) cold water. Return to a boil again, then reduce the heat to low and simmer until the filling is cooked through, about 5 minutes. Using a slotted spoon, transfer the wontons to the simmering broth. Add the spinach and simmer until it wilts, about 1 minute.

❀ To serve, ladle into 6 large warmed bowls, dividing the wontons evenly.

NUTRITIONAL ANALYSIS PER SERVING: Calories 207 (Kilojoules 1,709); Protein 24 g; Carbohydrates 51 g; Total Fat 11 g; Saturated Fat 4 g; Cholesterol 100 mg; Sodium 847 mg; Dietary Fiber 3 g

Beef Barley Soup

PREP TIME: 40 MINUTES

COOKING TIME: 2 HOURS

INGREDIENTS

3 lb (1.5 kg) meaty beef or veal
shanks

3 large yellow onions, chopped

6 carrots, peeled and chopped

4 celery stalks, chopped

1 cup (8 fl oz/250 ml) tomato purée

1 cup (8 oz/250 g) barley

6 tablespoons (3 oz/90 g) unsalted
butter

1 lb (500 g) fresh cremini mushrooms,
brushed clean and sliced

½ teaspoon minced garlic

salt and ground pepper to taste

4 tablespoons (⅓ oz/10 g) chopped
fresh dill

¼ cup (⅓ oz/10 g) chopped fresh
flat-leaf (Italian) parsley

6 tablespoons (3 fl oz/90 ml) sour
cream (optional)

A garnish of sour cream and chopped dill gives this hearty soup
a Russian flavor. Serve with dark rye bread for a complete meal.

SERVES 6

❀ Place the shanks in a saucepan and add water to cover generously.
Bring to a boil over high heat, skimming often to remove any foam
that forms on the surface. Add about two-thirds of the chopped onions,
the carrots, and the celery, reduce the heat to low, and cook, uncovered,
for about 1 hour. Add the tomato purée and the barley, cover partially,
and continue to cook over low heat until the barley is tender, about
1 hour longer.

❀ While the soup is cooking, in a large sauté pan over medium heat,
melt the butter. Add the remaining chopped onions and sauté, stirring
occasionally, until pale gold, 10–12 minutes. Raise the heat to high, add
the mushrooms, and sauté, stirring often, until softened, 6–8 minutes.
Add the garlic, reduce the heat to medium, and sauté until soft but not
brown, about 3 minutes longer. Season with salt, pepper, and 2 tablespoons of the dill.

❀ Remove the shanks from the pan and, when cool enough to handle,
cut the meat from the bone. Chop and reserve the meat; you should
have about 1⅓ cups (8 oz/250 g).

❀ Add the mushroom mixture and the reserved beef to the pan and stir
to heat through. Season with salt and pepper.

❀ Ladle into warmed bowls and sprinkle with the remaining 2 tablespoons dill and the parsley. Top each serving with a dollop of sour
cream, if desired.

NUTRITIONAL ANALYSIS PER SERVING: Calories 457 (Kilojoules 1,919); Protein 23 g;
Carbohydrates 54 g; Total Fat 19 g; Saturated Fat 10 g; Cholesterol 61 mg; Sodium 275 mg;
Dietary Fiber 13 g

Stuffed-Cabbage Soup

PREP TIME: 40 MINUTES

COOKING TIME: 1½ HOURS

INGREDIENTS

2 medium-large heads green cabbage,
1½–2 lb (750 g–1 kg) each, cored

FILLING

2 eggs

1 yellow onion, chopped

2 cloves garlic, minced

1½ lb (750 g) ground (minced) beef

2 cups (14 oz/440 g) long-grain
white rice

½ cup (3 oz/90 g) raisins, plumped in
hot water and drained

¼ cup (1¼ oz/37 g) pine nuts

¼ cup (⅓ oz/10 g) chopped fresh
parsley

¼ teaspoon ground allspice or
½ teaspoon ground cinnamon

salt and ground pepper to taste

7 cups (56 fl oz/1.75 l) Beef Stock
(page 12) or Chicken Stock
(page 11), or as needed

1 yellow onion, chopped

1 cup (6 oz/185 g) peeled, seeded,
and chopped tomatoes (fresh or
canned)

3 tablespoons chopped fresh flat-leaf
(Italian) parsley

3 tablespoons chopped fresh dill

This may seem like a great deal of work, but you will end up with a wonderful meal in a bowl with only good rye bread needed alongside. The raw rice in the stuffing mixture swells and cooks as the cabbage rolls poach in the stock.

SERVES 6

❀ Bring a large pot two-thirds full of salted water to a boil and drop in 1 cabbage. Simmer until the leaves loosen and are pliable, about 10 minutes. Transfer the cabbage to a colander and, when cool enough to handle, pull off the nicest large leaves. Repeat with the remaining cabbage head. You'll need about 18 leaves, or a few more if you want leftovers. Set the leaves aside. Reserve the remaining centers of the cabbage for another use.

❀ To make the filling, in a blender or food processor, combine the eggs, onion, and garlic and purée. Transfer to a bowl and add the ground beef and rice. Mix well. Add the plumped raisins, pine nuts, and parsley and again mix well. Season with the allspice or cinnamon and salt and pepper.

❀ Place a heaping tablespoon or two of the filling on the lower third of each cabbage leaf. Fold in the sides, then roll up from the lower end and skewer closed with a toothpick. Repeat until all the filling is used.

❀ In a deep, wide saucepan over medium heat, combine the stock, onion, and tomatoes. Bring to a simmer and carefully drop in the cabbage rolls. When the stock begins to boil very gently again, cover and simmer until very tender and fragrant, about 1½ hours. Taste and adjust the seasonings.

❀ To serve, using a slotted spoon, remove the cabbage rolls and place 3 rolls in each individual warmed bowl, discarding the toothpicks as you do. Ladle the hot broth over the rolls. Garnish with the parsley and dill and serve at once.

NUTRITIONAL ANALYSIS PER SERVING: Calories 809 (Kilojoules 3,398); Protein 37 g; Carbohydrates 87 g; Total Fat 36 g; Saturated Fat 13 g; Cholesterol 167 mg; Sodium 230 mg; Dietary Fiber 10 g

Fresh Tomato Soup

PREP TIME: 20 MINUTES

COOKING TIME: 30 MINUTES

INGREDIENTS

¼ cup (2 oz/60 g) unsalted butter or
(2 fl oz/60 ml) olive oil

2 large yellow onions, chopped

3 tablespoons finely grated orange
zest (optional)

2 tablespoons peeled and grated
fresh ginger (optional)

pinch of ground cloves (optional)

12 large beefsteak or 18 regular
very ripe tomatoes, quartered

salt and ground pepper to taste

heavy (double) cream or milk
to taste (optional)

SERVING TIP: The soup can be gar-
nished in a variety of ways: chopped
fresh basil, flat-leaf (Italian) parsley,
or mint; a dollop of pesto or Avocado
Salsa (page 65); or a few garlic croutons
and a sprinkling of grated Parmesan
cheese. It can also be cooled, covered,
and refrigerated until well chilled
and served cold in chilled bowls.

This is the ideal summer soup. It does not call for stock, as the ripe tomatoes make their own wonderful "broth." Obviously, the success of this soup is dependent upon fully ripened, flavorful tomatoes, so don't try to make it without them.

SERVES 6–8

❀ In a heavy saucepan over medium heat, melt the butter or warm the oil. Add the onions and sauté, stirring occasionally, until tender and translucent, about 10 minutes. Stir in the orange zest, ginger, or cloves, if using, and cook for 3 minutes to blend the flavors. Then add the tomatoes and cook over medium heat, stirring occasionally to prevent scorching, until the tomatoes have completely broken down and have released a great deal of liquid, about 20 minutes. Remove from the heat.

❀ Working in batches, purée the soup in a blender or food processor. Pass the purée through a food mill or medium-mesh sieve placed over a clean saucepan to remove the peel and seeds. Reheat gently over medium-low heat. Season with salt and pepper. If the flavor is slightly acidic, add a little cream or milk.

❀ Ladle into warmed bowls and serve hot.

NUTRITIONAL ANALYSIS PER SERVING: Calories 164 (Kilojoules 689); Protein 4 g; Carbohydrates 24 g; Total Fat 8 g; Saturated Fat 4 g; Cholesterol 18 mg; Sodium 38 mg; Dietary Fiber 6 g

Matzo Ball Soup

PREP TIME: 20 MINUTES, PLUS
1 HOUR FOR CHILLING

COOKING TIME: 1 HOUR

INGREDIENTS

10–12 cups (2½–3 qt/2.5–3 l) Chicken Stock (page 11)

4 eggs

⅓ cup (3 fl oz/80 ml) tap water or seltzer water

3 tablespoons rendered chicken fat or melted and cooled margarine

½ teaspoon salt, plus salt to taste

¼ teaspoon ground white pepper, plus white pepper to taste

1¼ cups (7 oz/220 g) matzo meal

2 cups (12 oz/375 g) diced cooked chicken (optional)

1 cup (5 oz/155 g) diced cooked carrots (optional)

1 cup (5 oz/155 g) shelled English peas (optional)

¼ cup (⅓ oz/10 g) chopped fresh parsley

MAKE-AHEAD TIP: The matzo balls can be cooked several hours in advance and reheated in the soup just before serving. Be sure to simmer them long enough so that they are heated all the way through.

Matzo ball soup is not just for Passover. It is heartwarming during the chilly days of fall and winter, when a substantial soup is needed. If you use canned broth for this soup, use just 6 cups (48 fl oz/1.5 l) and skip the first step of reducing the stock. Canned broth becomes far too salty when reduced. Look for matzo meal and jars of rendered chicken fat in the Jewish food sections of most supermarkets or in Jewish delis.

SERVES 6

❋ In a saucepan over high heat, bring the stock to a boil. Boil, uncovered, until reduced to about 6 cups (48 fl oz/1.5 l), about 30 minutes.

❋ In a large bowl, whisk together lightly the eggs and tap or seltzer water. Add the chicken fat or margarine and stir until the fat is mixed in. Add the ½ teaspoon salt and the ¼ teaspoon white pepper. Gradually pour in the matzo meal, adding it in a steady stream while stirring with a spoon. Do not overbeat. Cover and chill for 30 minutes.

❋ Line 2 large baking sheets with parchment (baking) paper. Using a large soup spoon dipped in cold water and wet hands, form the chilled matzo mixture into balls about 1½ inches (4 cm) in diameter. Do not roll too compactly. Place on the prepared baking sheets, cover, and refrigerate for at least 30 minutes or up to 3 hours or until ready to cook.

❋ Bring 2 large saucepans three-fourths full of salted water to a boil over high heat. Drop in the matzo balls, cover the pans, and allow the water to return to a boil. Immediately reduce the heat to low and simmer until doubled in size and cooked through, 30–40 minutes. To test, cut into a ball; it should be cooked uniformly to the center. Using a slotted spoon, transfer to a plate and set aside.

❋ Season the reduced stock with salt and pepper, bring to a boil, and then reduce the heat to low so that it simmers. Add the matzo balls and the chicken, carrots, and/or peas, if using. Simmer until all the ingredients are heated through, 8–10 minutes.

❋ To serve, ladle into warmed bowls, dividing the matzo balls evenly, and sprinkle with the parsley.

NUTRITIONAL ANALYSIS PER SERVING: Calories 286 (Kilojoules 1,201); Protein 12 g; Carbohydrates 30 g; Total Fat 12 g; Saturated Fat 4 g; Cholesterol 153 mg; Sodium 408 mg; Dietary Fiber 0 g

Asparagus Soup

PREP TIME: 15 MINUTES

COOKING TIME: 30 MINUTES

INGREDIENTS

2½ lb (1.25 kg) asparagus, tough ends removed

¼ cup (2 oz/60 g) unsalted butter

1½ cups (7½ oz/235 g) peeled and diced russet potato

4–5 cups (32–40 fl oz/1–1.25 l) Vegetable Stock (page 13) or Chicken Stock (page 11)

about ½ cup (4 fl oz/125 ml) milk or heavy (double) cream (optional)

salt and ground pepper to taste

3 tablespoons chopped fresh flat-leaf (Italian) parsley or mint

PREP TIP: Look for asparagus with tightly closed tips. When the tips start to open, it is a sign that the asparagus are no longer at their peak and are less sweet. They will give the soup a grassy taste. The richness of the added cream will help balance that flavor.

The addition of potato and only a little milk or cream offers a light richness to this satisfying soup. Chopped toasted hazelnuts (filberts) and chopped fresh parsley, toasted pine nuts or chopped almonds, or whipped cream flavored with grated lemon zest can be used in place of the parsley or mint garnish.

SERVES 6

❀ Cut 1 inch (2.5 cm) off the tips of the asparagus spears. Set aside. Cut the remaining asparagus into 2-inch (5-cm) lengths. Bring a large saucepan three-fourths full of salted water to a boil. Add the asparagus tips and parboil for 2 minutes. Drain and immediately immerse the tips in cold water to halt the cooking. Drain, pat dry with paper towels, and set aside.

❀ In a large saucepan over medium heat, melt the butter. Add all the asparagus except the tips and sauté, stirring occasionally, until well coated with the butter, 2–3 minutes. Add the potato and about 3 cups (24 fl oz/ 750 ml) of the stock or just enough to cover the asparagus. Cover the pan, bring to a boil, then reduce the heat to low, and simmer until the asparagus and the potato are very tender and just about falling apart, about 20 minutes. Remove from the heat.

❀ Working in batches, purée the soup in a blender or food processor. Return the purée to a clean saucepan and add the remaining 1–2 cups (8–16 fl oz/250–500 ml) stock as needed to achieve the desired consistency. Then add the milk or cream if a little richness is desired. Reheat gently over low heat, adding the reserved asparagus tips. Season with salt and pepper.

❀ Ladle the soup into warmed bowls and sprinkle with the parsley or mint. Serve at once.

NUTRITIONAL ANALYSIS PER SERVING: Calories 147 (Kilojoules 617); Protein 6 g; Carbohydrates 16 g; Total Fat 8 g; Saturated Fat 5 g; Cholesterol 21 mg; Sodium 16 mg; Dietary Fiber 3 g

Asian Shrimp and Noodle Soup

PREP TIME: 25 MINUTES

COOKING TIME: 15 MINUTES

INGREDIENTS

½–1 lb (250–500 g) fresh Chinese egg noodles

vegetable oil for tossing noodles, plus 2 tablespoons

5 green (spring) onions, cut up, plus 2 tablespoons minced

2 shallots

2 cloves garlic

1 lemongrass stalk, tender base portion only, cut into small pieces

1 jalapeño chile, cut up

2 tablespoons peeled and thinly sliced fresh ginger

9 cups (72 fl oz/2.25 l) Chicken Stock (page 11) or canned low-sodium broth simmered with 3–4 slices peeled fresh ginger for 10–15 minutes

1 tablespoon grated lime zest

1 lb (500 g) shrimp (prawns), peeled, deveined, and halved lengthwise

¼ lb (125 g) fresh white mushrooms, brushed clean and thinly sliced

¼ lb (125 g) snow peas (mangetouts), cut lengthwise into ½-inch (12-mm) strips

2 cups (4 oz/125 g) bean sprouts or 2 cups (2 oz/60 g) spinach leaves, stems removed and thinly sliced

2 tablespoons lime juice

salt and ground pepper to taste

2 tablespoons each finely shredded fresh basil and mint

This soup can be as opulent as you like. Add additional shellfish or just increase the amount of shrimp. Snow peas, bean sprouts, mushrooms, and spinach are all at your disposal for a more or less filling meal. The amount of stock you need will be determined by how many noodles you add to the soup.

SERVES 6

❀ Bring a large saucepan three-fourths full of salted water to a boil. Add the noodles, stir well, and parboil for 1–2 minutes. Drain and toss with a bit of vegetable oil. Set aside.

❀ In a food processor, combine the green onions, shallots, garlic, lemongrass, jalapeño chile (include some of the seeds), and ginger. Pulse until a paste forms.

❀ In a saucepan over medium heat, warm the 2 tablespoons vegetable oil. Add the paste and cook, stirring often, until fragrant, about 5 minutes. Add the stock and the lime zest and simmer for 5 minutes to infuse the stock with the flavors. Add the parboiled noodles, shrimp, mushrooms, snow peas, and bean sprouts or spinach, and simmer until the shrimp turn pink, about 4 minutes. Season with the lime juice, salt, and pepper.

❀ Stir in the basil, mint, and minced green onions, and immediately ladle into warmed soup bowls. Serve hot.

NUTRITIONAL ANALYSIS PER SERVING: Calories 409 (Kilojoules 1,718); Protein 27 g; Carbohydrates 52 g; Total Fat 11 g; Saturated Fat 2 g; Cholesterol 153 mg; Sodium 257 mg; Dietary Fiber 3 g

Chicken, Tortilla, and Lime Soup

PREP TIME: 25 MINUTES

COOKING TIME: 50 MINUTES

INGREDIENTS

4 quarts (4 l) Chicken Stock (page 11)

vegetable oil for deep-frying

3 corn tortillas, cut into strips
   2 inches (5 cm) long

1¼ lb (625 g) boneless, skinless
   chicken breasts

3 tablespoons olive oil

1 large yellow onion, chopped

2 tablespoons minced garlic

2–3 teaspoons finely minced
   jalapeño chile, with or without
   seeds to taste

1½ cups (9 oz/280 g) peeled, seeded,
   and diced tomatoes (fresh or
   canned)

6 tablespoons (¼ oz/7 g) chopped
   fresh cilantro (fresh coriander)

6 tablespoons (3 fl oz/90 ml) fresh
   lime juice

1½ teaspoons salt, or to taste

½ teaspoon ground pepper

12 paper-thin lime slices, cut into
   quarters

In this classic soup, called *sopa de lima*, from Mexico's Yucatán region, the chicken is not cooked directly in the stock because it will make it cloudy. Be careful not to add too much chile or the soup may be too fiery for comfort. You want to maintain a good balance between the tartness of the lime and the heat of the chiles. One large avocado, halved, pitted, peeled, and diced, makes a soothing garnish to the spicy broth. Although it's not authentic, 1 cup (6 oz/185 g) corn kernels may be added to the soup with the tomatoes.

SERVES 6

❀ In a large saucepan over high heat, bring 3½ quarts (3.5 l) of the stock to a boil. Reduce the heat so the stock boils gently and boil until reduced by half to about 7 cups (56 fl oz/1.75 l), about 30 minutes.

❀ Meanwhile, pour vegetable oil into a deep frying pan to a depth of 2 inches (5 cm) and heat to 375°F (190°C) on a deep-frying thermometer. Working in batches, drop in the tortilla strips and fry until golden and crisp, about 2 minutes. Using a slotted spoon, transfer the fried tortilla strips to paper towels to drain.

❀ In a saucepan, combine the chicken breasts with the remaining 2 cups (16 fl oz/500 ml) stock. Bring to a simmer and cook gently until the chicken is opaque throughout when cut into with a knife, about 8 minutes. Transfer to a cutting board and, when cool enough to handle, cut the chicken breasts into bite-sized pieces. Set aside. Discard the stock or reserve for another use. If not using immediately, cover and refrigerate.

❀ In a large saucepan over medium heat, warm the olive oil. Add the onion and sauté, stirring occasionally, until tender and translucent, about 10 minutes. Add the garlic and jalapeño chile and cook for 1–2 minutes to soften. Add the reduced stock, raise the heat to high, and bring to a boil. Reduce the heat to low, add the cooked chicken, the tomatoes, cilantro, lime juice, salt, and pepper, and simmer until the chicken is heated through, about 5 minutes. Taste and adjust the seasonings.

❀ Ladle the hot soup into warmed bowls. Sprinkle the lime pieces and tortilla strips evenly over the tops. Serve immediately.

NUTRITIONAL ANALYSIS PER SERVING: Calories 321 (Kilojoules 1,348); Protein 31 g; Carbohydrates 19 g; Total Fat 14 g; Saturated Fat 3 g; Cholesterol 64 mg; Sodium 919 mg; Dietary Fiber 2 g

Fresh Corn Soup

PREP TIME: 30 MINUTES

COOKING TIME: 30 MINUTES

INGREDIENTS

2 red bell peppers (capsicums) or
  3 poblano chiles (optional)

lemon juice to taste (optional)

¼ cup (2 oz/60 g) unsalted butter

I yellow onion, diced

kernels from 10 ears of corn, 8–10
  cups (3–3¾ lb/1.5–1.75 kg)

6 cups (48 fl oz/1.5 l) water or
  Chicken Stock (page 11), or
  as needed

salt and ground pepper to taste

sugar to taste, if needed

shredded Monterey jack cheese
  (optional)

COOKING TIP: For soup with a more intense corn flavor, use a stock made from the leftover corncobs instead of the water or chicken stock. Cut each cob into 3 or 4 pieces and put in a saucepan with water or stock to cover. Bring to a boil over high heat, reduce the heat to medium, and simmer, uncovered, for 30 minutes. Strain and reserve the liquid. You will need about 6 cups (48 fl oz/1.5 l).

Sometimes the early summer white corn is so sweet you think that sugar has been added. For this recipe, you may want to combine white corn for sweetness and yellow corn for body.

SERVES 6

❋ Preheat a broiler (griller). If using bell peppers, cut in half lengthwise and remove the skin, seeds, and ribs. Place, cut sides down, on a baking sheet. Broil (grill) until the skins blacken and blister. If using chiles, broil (grill) them whole, turning as necessary to blacken evenly. Remove from the broiler, drape the peppers or chiles loosely with aluminum foil, let cool for 10 minutes, and then peel away the skins. If using the chiles, slit lengthwise and remove and discard the stems and seeds. Purée or chop them (you will need to chop if you plan on using jack cheese as well) and reserve for garnishing. If using bell peppers, purée in a blender or food processor and season with a little lemon juice, if desired. Reserve for garnishing the soup.

❋ In a large saucepan over medium heat, melt the butter. Add the onion and sauté, stirring occasionally, until tender and translucent, about 10 minutes. Add the corn, stir well, and cook for 2 minutes to blend with the onion. Pour in the water or chicken stock; it should just barely cover the corn. Raise the heat to high and bring to a boil. Reduce the heat to medium and simmer, uncovered, until the corn is tender, about 6 minutes. Remove from the heat and let cool slightly.

❋ Working in batches, purée the soup in the blender. Then pass the purée through a food mill fitted with the coarse disc or a coarse-mesh sieve placed over a clean saucepan. Place over medium-high heat and reheat to serving temperature. Season with salt, pepper, and with sugar, if needed. Add more stock if the soup is too thick.

❋ To serve, ladle into warmed bowls and top each with a swirl of the pepper purée and a little jack cheese, if desired.

NUTRITIONAL ANALYSIS PER SERVING: Calories 284 (Kilojoules 1,193); Protein 8 g; Carbohydrates 48 g; Total Fat 10 g; Saturated Fat 5 g; Cholesterol 21 mg; Sodium 231 mg; Dietary Fiber 8 g

New England Clam Chowder

PREP TIME: 20 MINUTES

COOKING TIME: 35 MINUTES

INGREDIENTS

5 lb (2.5 kg) littleneck or cherry-stone clams (48–60 clams), well scrubbed

about 2 cups (16 fl oz/500 ml) dry white wine, water, or Fish Stock (page 13)

about 3 cups (24 fl oz/750 ml) bottled clam juice or Fish Stock (page 13)

2 tablespoons olive oil

6 oz (185 g) pancetta or bacon, cut into small pieces

2 yellow onions, chopped

6–8 small red new potatoes, cut into small chunks

1½ cups (12 fl oz/375 ml) heavy (double) cream

ground black pepper to taste

pinch of cayenne pepper (optional)

2 tablespoons unsalted butter (optional)

¼ cup (⅓ oz/10 g) chopped fresh parsley or chives, or 2 tablespoons chopped fresh thyme

The smoky taste of bacon or the sweetness of pancetta adds a more refined touch than the salt pork traditionally used in New England–style chowder.

SERVES 6

✽ In a large, wide saucepan over high heat, combine the clams and the wine, water, or stock. Cover and cook until the clams open, about 5 minutes. Using a slotted spoon, transfer the clams to a bowl, discarding any that did not open. Strain the cooking liquid through a sieve lined with damp cheesecloth (muslin) placed over a large bowl. Remove the clams from their shells and chop coarsely, capturing and straining any of the juices. Measure the cooking liquid and add enough clam juice or fish stock to measure 5 cups (40 fl oz/1.25 l). Set aside.

✽ In a saucepan over medium-low heat, warm the olive oil. Add the pancetta or bacon and onions and cook, stirring occasionally to prevent sticking, until softened, about 10 minutes. Raise the heat to high, add the reserved liquid, and bring to a boil. Add the potatoes and reduce the heat to low. Cook, uncovered, until the potatoes are firm but almost completely cooked through, 10–15 minutes. Add the clams and simmer until heated through, about 4 minutes. Add the cream and season with the black pepper and the cayenne pepper, if using. Swirl in the butter, if using, and top with the chopped herbs.

✽ Ladle into warmed individual bowls and serve immediately.

NUTRITIONAL ANALYSIS PER SERVING: Calories 573 (Kilojoules 2,407); Protein 14 g; Carbohydrates 19 g; Total Fat 44 g; Saturated Fat 20 g; Cholesterol 120 mg; Sodium 948 mg; Dietary Fiber 2 g

COOKING TIP: In the summer, you may want to add about 2 cups (12 oz/375 g) corn kernels when you add the clams. You can also add chunks of lobster, fish, or bay scallops to this chowder.

Black Bean Soup

PREP TIME: 30 MINUTES,
    PLUS 1 HOUR FOR SOAKING
    BEANS

COOKING TIME: 1½ HOURS

INGREDIENTS

3 cups (21 oz/655 g) dried black beans

8 cups (64 fl oz/2 l) water

1 ham bone or ham hock

2 tablespoons olive oil

2 yellow onions, chopped

4 cloves garlic, minced

1 tablespoon ground cumin

½ teaspoon ground cinnamon

¼ teaspoon ground cloves

1–2 tablespoons sherry vinegar

salt and ground pepper to taste

AVOCADO SALSA

1 large or 2 medium avocados,
    halved, pitted, peeled, and diced

½ cup (3 oz/90 g) seeded and diced
    tomato

¼ cup (1¼ oz/37 g) finely diced red
    (Spanish) onion

chopped fresh cilantro (fresh
    coriander) (optional)

1 small clove garlic, minced

½ small jalapeño chile, minced

2 tablespoons lime or lemon juice,
    or to taste

salt to taste

A shot of dry sherry and a garnish of paper-thin lemon slices are classic additions to Spanish black bean soup. But black bean soup is versatile. Here, ground cumin and cinnamon and a garnish of avocado salsa give it a Latin American accent.

SERVES 8

❈ Pick over the beans and discard any misshapen beans or stones. Rinse the beans, drain, and place in a saucepan. Add water to cover and bring to a boil over high heat. Boil for 2 minutes, then remove from the heat, cover, and let stand for 1 hour.

❈ Drain the beans and return to the saucepan. Add the 8 cups (64 fl oz/ 2 l) water and the ham bone or ham hock. Bring to a boil over high heat. Cover partially, reduce the heat to low, and simmer.

❈ Once the beans are simmering, in a large sauté pan over medium heat, warm the olive oil. Add the onions and sauté, stirring occasionally, until tender and translucent, about 10 minutes. Add the garlic, cumin, cinnamon, and cloves and cook for about 2 minutes longer. Add the onion mixture to the beans and simmer until very tender, 1–1½ hours; the timing will depend upon the age of the beans.

❈ Remove the soup from the heat. Remove the ham bone or ham hock and discard. Working in batches, purée the soup in a blender (or pass through a food mill). Return the soup to a clean saucepan and season with sherry vinegar and salt and pepper. Gradually reheat over medium heat, stirring often to prevent scorching. Thin with water if the soup is too thick, then taste and adjust the seasonings; it will probably need a little more salt.

❈ Just before serving the soup, make the salsa: In a bowl, combine the avocados, tomato, onion, cilantro (if using), garlic, chile, lime or lemon juice, and salt. Toss well.

❈ Ladle the soup into warmed individual bowls. Top each serving with a spoonful of the salsa, and serve at once.

NUTRITIONAL ANALYSIS PER SERVING: Calories 367 (Kilojoules 1,541); Protein 18 g; Carbohydrates 55 g; Total Fat 10 g; Saturated Fat 1 g; Cholesterol 0 mg; Sodium 344 mg; Dietary Fiber 11 g

Bread and Onion Soup

PREP TIME: 20 MINUTES

COOKING TIME: 1¾ HOURS

INGREDIENTS

¼ cup (2 oz/60 g) unsalted butter

6 large yellow onions, thinly sliced

6 tablespoons (¾ oz/20 g) chopped fresh basil

5 cups (40 fl oz/1.25 l) water, Vegetable Stock *(page 13)*, or Chicken Stock *(page 11)*

salt and ground pepper to taste

4 thick (1-inch/2.5-cm) slices coarse country bread, preferably day-old, cut into 1-inch (2.5-cm) cubes

½ cup (2 oz/60 g) grated Parmesan or shredded fontina cheese

PREP TIP: If you must use fresh bread, toast it first to crisp it and concentrate its flavor.

Good-quality coarse country bread is essential for making this soup. Ideally, the bread should be a day old, as a drier loaf will absorb more liquid.

SERVES 6

❁ In a large sauté pan over low heat, melt the butter. Add the onions and sauté very slowly, stirring often, until caramelized, about 45 minutes. The onions must be sweet and golden but not brown. Stir in 2 tablespoons of the basil and cook for 5 minutes to flavor the onions. Add the water or stock, cover, and simmer until the onions are quite tender, about 30 minutes longer.

❁ Meanwhile, preheat an oven to 350°F (180°C).

❁ When the onion mixture is ready, season with salt and pepper and remove from the heat. Place individual ovenproof bowls on 1 or 2 baking sheets and evenly divide the bread cubes among them. Top with the hot onion mixture and then the cheese.

❁ Bake until the cheese melts and the soup is piping hot, 10–20 minutes. Garnish with the remaining basil and serve.

NUTRITIONAL ANALYSIS PER SERVING: Calories 283 (Kilojoules 1,189); Protein 9 g; Carbohydrates 37 g; Total Fat 7 g; Saturated Fat 7 g; Cholesterol 27 mg; Sodium 362 mg; Dietary Fiber 5 g

Hearty Split-Pea Soup

PREP TIME: 15 MINUTES

COOKING TIME: 1¼ HOURS

INGREDIENTS

2 cups (14 oz/440 g) dried split peas

2 tablespoons unsalted butter

1 large yellow onion, chopped

2 carrots, peeled and chopped

1 bay leaf

6 cups (48 fl oz/1.5 l) water or Chicken Stock (page 11), or as needed

½ lb (250 g) spinach, tough stems removed and finely chopped

3 slices bacon or pancetta (optional)

milk for thinning (optional)

1 teaspoon salt

½ teaspoon ground pepper

SERVING TIP: For a more festive split-pea soup, add a few tablespoons of champagne to each bowl, garnish with a generous spoonful of whipped cream flavored with lemon juice and grated lemon zest, and then top with the crumbled bacon or pancetta.

Chopped spinach and a sprinkling of crumbled, crisply cooked bacon or pancetta bring robust flavor and texture to this satisfying soup.

SERVES 4–6

❋ Pick over the split peas and discard any misshapen peas or stones. Rinse the split peas and drain.

❋ In a saucepan over medium heat, melt the butter. Add the onion and sauté, stirring occasionally, until tender and translucent, about 10 minutes. Add the split peas, carrots, bay leaf, and 6 cups (48 fl oz/1.5 l) water or stock. Raise the heat to high and bring to a boil. Cover, reduce the heat to low, and simmer until the peas are very soft, 45 minutes. If the mixture seems too thick, add more water or stock as needed.

❋ Discard the bay leaf. Add the spinach and simmer until it wilts, about 3 minutes.

❋ Meanwhile, if using the bacon or pancetta, place a frying pan over medium heat. Add the bacon or pancetta slices and fry, turning as needed, until crisp, about 7 minutes. Transfer to paper towels to drain. When cool, crumble.

❋ Remove the soup from the heat and let cool slightly. Working in batches, purée in a blender or food processor. Return to a clean saucepan and add milk, water, or stock as needed to thin to desired consistency. Place over medium-high heat and reheat to serving temperature. Season with the salt and pepper.

❋ To serve, ladle into warmed bowls and sprinkle with the crumbled bacon or pancetta, if using.

NUTRITIONAL ANALYSIS PER SERVING: Calories 349 (Kilojoules 1,466); Protein 21 g; Carbohydrates 56 g; Total Fat 6 g; Saturated Fat 3 g; Cholesterol 13 mg; Sodium 516 mg; Dietary Fiber 7 g

Creamy Mushroom Soup

PREP TIME: 30 MINUTES, PLUS
1 HOUR FOR SOAKING
MUSHROOMS

COOKING TIME: 45 MINUTES

INGREDIENTS

1 oz (30 g) dried porcini

1 cup (8 fl oz/250 ml) hot water

6 tablespoons (3 oz/90 g) unsalted butter

2 yellow onions, chopped

2 lb (1 kg) fresh mushrooms (see note), brushed clean and thinly sliced

5 cups (40 fl oz/1.25 l) Chicken Stock (page 11)

¼ cup (2 fl oz/60 ml) dry sherry or Madeira wine

1 cup (8 fl oz/250 ml) heavy (double) cream

salt and ground pepper to taste

ground nutmeg to taste

3 tablespoons chopped fresh flat-leaf (Italian) parsley

COOKING TIP: For an Italian-style mushroom soup, omit the sherry and cream. Use Beef Stock (page 12) or Chicken Stock (page 11) and add 2 tablespoons tomato paste to the sautéed onions. Garnish the soup with croutons and grated Parmesan cheese.

Serve this soup in the fall, when mushrooms are in abundance. Although fresh wild mushrooms such as chanterelles or porcini make for a particularly earthy and interesting soup, you can also make a delicious soup using cultivated white mushrooms, cremini, portobellos, or a combination.

SERVES 6

❀ Rinse the dried porcini and place in a bowl. Add the hot water and let stand for about 1 hour. Lift out the porcini, squeezing them over the bowl to remove as much moisture as possible, and chop finely. Strain the soaking liquid through a sieve lined with damp cheesecloth (muslin) into a pitcher or bowl and set aside.

❀ In a heavy saucepan over low heat, melt 2 tablespoons of the butter. Add the onions and sauté, stirring occasionally, until translucent and tender, about 10 minutes. Remove from the heat but leave in the pan.

❀ In a large, wide sauté pan over medium heat, melt the remaining 4 tablespoons (2 oz/60 g) butter. Add the fresh mushrooms and cook slowly, stirring occasionally, until they give off their juices and soften, 10–15 minutes. If you like a coarser-textured soup, set aside about 1 cup (3 oz/90 g) of the mushrooms to use as a garnish; keep warm.

❀ Add the mushrooms in the sauté pan, the chopped porcini, and the strained mushroom liquid to the sautéed onions and return the pan to medium-high heat. Pour in the stock and bring to a boil. Reduce the heat to low and simmer, uncovered, until the stock is infused with the flavors, about 20 minutes.

❀ Working in batches and using a slotted spoon, transfer the mushrooms and onions to a blender or food processor. Add just a little of the cooking liquid and purée until smooth. Transfer to a clean saucepan. Thin the purée with as much of the remaining liquid as needed. Add the sherry or Madeira and cream and season with salt, pepper, and nutmeg. Reheat gently over low heat.

❀ Ladle into warmed bowls. If you have set aside mushrooms for garnish, divide them among the bowls, then sprinkle with the parsley.

NUTRITIONAL ANALYSIS PER SERVING: Calories 352 (Kilojoules 1,478); Protein 8 g; Carbohydrates 17 g; Total Fat 28 g; Saturated Fat 17 g; Cholesterol 88 mg; Sodium 104 mg; Dietary Fiber 4 g

Ribollita

PREP TIME: 30 MINUTES,
PLUS 1 HOUR FOR
SOAKING BEANS

COOKING TIME: 4 HOURS, PLUS
8 HOURS FOR CHILLING

INGREDIENTS

WHITE BEANS

1½ cups (10½ oz/330 g) dried white
   beans, preferably cannellini

4 cups (32 fl oz/1 l) water

1 yellow onion

2 cloves garlic

1 bay leaf

2 teaspoons salt

½ cup (4 fl oz/125 ml) extra-virgin
   olive oil, plus more for drizzling

2 yellow onions, chopped

4 celery stalks, chopped

3 carrots, peeled and chopped

2 cloves garlic, minced

1 cup (6 oz/185 g) chopped canned
   plum (Roma) tomatoes

1–2 tablespoons tomato paste

1 lb (500 g) Savoy cabbage or ⅓ lb
   (155 g) each kale, Swiss chard,
   and Savoy cabbage, tough stems
   removed and leaves coarsely
   chopped or shredded

1 tablespoon chopped fresh thyme

salt and ground pepper to taste

6–8 slices coarse country bread

Ribollita is Italian for "reboiled." First you make a hearty Tuscan vegetable soup, which is refrigerated overnight. The next day, you reheat ("reboil") the soup with slices of bread in it, which break down and thicken it further.

SERVES 6

❊ Pick over the beans, discarding any misshapen beans and stones. Rinse well and place in a saucepan with the water. Bring to a boil over high heat, boil for 2 minutes, then cover and remove from the heat. Let stand for 1 hour. Drain and return to the saucepan with fresh water to cover by about 2 inches (5 cm). Add the onion, garlic, and bay leaf and bring to a boil over high heat. Reduce the heat to low and simmer, uncovered, until the beans are tender but not falling apart, about 1 hour. Add the salt during the last 10 minutes of cooking. Remove and discard the onion, garlic, and bay leaf. Set the beans aside in their liquid.

❊ In a large saucepan over medium heat, warm the ½ cup (4 fl oz/125 ml) olive oil. Add the onions, celery, carrots, and garlic and sauté, stirring occasionally, until the onions are tender and translucent, about 10 minutes. Add the chopped tomatoes and tomato paste and cook, stirring occasionally, for 5 minutes. Add the cabbage or mixed greens, the cooked white beans and their liquid, the thyme, the salt and pepper, and enough water just to cover the vegetables. Raise the heat to medium-high and bring to a boil. Cover, reduce the heat to low, and simmer until all the vegetables are very tender, about 2 hours. Remove from the heat, let cool, cover, and refrigerate for 8 hours or for up to 3 days.

❊ Remove the soup from the refrigerator. Layer 2 or 3 bread slices in the bottom of a large, heavy-bottomed saucepan. Ladle in enough soup just to cover. Repeat the layers until all the bread and soup are in the pan, ending with the soup. Slowly bring the soup to a boil over low heat, stirring often to make sure that the bottom doesn't scorch and to break up the bread, 20–30 minutes. It should eventually dissolve and absorb the liquids completely, forming a very thick soup.

❊ Scoop into warmed bowls and drizzle with the olive oil. Serve at once.

NUTRITIONAL ANALYSIS PER SERVING: Calories 621 (Kilojoules 2,608); Protein 18 g; Carbohydrates 66 g; Total Fat 35 g; Saturated Fat 5 g; Cholesterol 0 mg; Sodium 1123 mg; Dietary Fiber 9 g

Roasted Eggplant Soup

PREP TIME: 15 MINUTES, PLUS
30 MINUTES FOR DRAINING

COOKING TIME: 1 HOUR, 20
MINUTES

INGREDIENTS

3 eggplants (aubergines)

3 tablespoons unsalted butter or
olive oil

I large yellow onion, chopped

2 cloves garlic, minced

1–2 tablespoons peeled and grated
fresh ginger (optional)

5 cups (40 fl oz/1.25 l) Chicken
Stock (page 11) or Vegetable
Stock (page 13), plus extra for
thinning (optional)

½ cup (4 fl oz/125 ml) heavy (double)
cream (optional)

salt and ground pepper to taste

WHIPPED CREAM GARNISH
¾ cup (6 fl oz/180 ml) heavy (double)
cream

grated zest and juice of I lemon

3 tablespoons chopped fresh flat-leaf
(Italian) parsley

SERVING TIP: In the summer, garnish
this soup with chopped tomatoes
and basil or a dollop of pesto. In the
fall, try roasted red pepper purée,
and in the winter, chopped oil-packed
sun-dried tomatoes mixed with
thyme or mint.

Roasting the eggplants rather than sautéing them reduces the amount of oil needed for this recipe and gives the soup a deeper, richer flavor.

SERVES 6

✳ Preheat an oven to 450°F (230°C).

✳ Using a fork, prick the eggplants in a few places and place on a baking sheet. Bake, turning once or twice to ensure even cooking, until very tender, about 1 hour. Remove from the oven and, when cool enough to handle, cut in half and scoop out the flesh from the skins into a colander, discarding any large pockets of seeds. Place the colander in the sink and let the eggplant pulp drain to rid it of bitter juices, 20–30 minutes. Coarsely chop the pulp and set aside.

✳ In a saucepan over medium heat, melt the butter or warm the oil. Add the onion and sauté, stirring occasionally, until tender and translucent, about 10 minutes. Add the garlic and the ginger, if using, and sauté until fragrant, about 2 minutes. Add the eggplant pulp and 5 cups (40 fl oz/1.25 l) stock, raise the heat to high, and bring to a boil. Reduce the heat to low and simmer for a few minutes to meld the flavors. Remove from the heat and let cool slightly.

✳ Working in batches, purée the soup in a blender or food processor and return to a clean saucepan. Reheat gently, thinning to the desired consistency with additional stock or with the ½ cup (4 fl oz/125 ml) cream, if the eggplant is acidic or sharp in flavor. Season with salt and pepper.

✳ In a bowl, beat the ¾ cup (6 fl oz/180 ml) cream just until soft peaks form. Fold in the lemon zest and juice.

✳ Ladle the soup into warmed individual bowls and garnish with a dollop of the whipped cream and a sprinkling of parsley. Serve hot.

NUTRITIONAL ANALYSIS PER SERVING: Calories 262 (Kilojoules 1,100); Protein 6 g; Carbohydrates 23 g; Total Fat 18 g; Saturated Fat 11 g; Cholesterol 59 mg; Sodium 103 mg; Dietary Fiber 5 g

Brazilian Shellfish Soup

PREP TIME: 40 MINUTES

COOKING TIME: 30 MINUTES

INGREDIENTS

¼ cup (2 oz/60 g) unsalted butter

3 yellow onions, chopped

2 jalapeño chiles, minced

¼ cup (1 oz/30 g) ground dry-roasted
   peanuts or cashews (optional)

4 cloves garlic, minced

2 tablespoons peeled and grated
   fresh ginger

1 tablespoon ground coriander

4–5 cups (32–40 fl oz/1–1.25 l) Fish
   Stock (page 13)

2 cups (12 oz/375 g) peeled, seeded,
   and chopped plum (Roma) tomatoes

½ cup (4 fl oz/125 ml) coconut milk

¼ teaspoon saffron threads, steeped
   in ¼ cup (2 fl oz/60 ml) white wine

¼ cup (⅓ oz/10 g) chopped fresh
   cilantro (fresh coriander)

2–3 tablespoons lemon or lime juice

salt and ground pepper to taste

1½ lb (750 g) firm white fish fillets,
   cut into 1½-inch (4-cm) chunks

18 each mussels, well scrubbed and
   debearded; shrimp (prawns),
   shelled and deveined with tails
   intact; and sea scallops

about 6 cups (30 oz/940 g) hot,
   cooked white rice

3 tablespoons chopped fresh
   cilantro (fresh coriander)

3 tablespoons shredded dried
   coconut, toasted

This soup combines some of the most vibrant flavors of the Brazilian pantry: coconut, tomatoes, garlic, lemon juice, cilantro, cayenne, peanuts, and saffron. If you like, add chunks of meat from 2 small lobsters or 1 Dungeness crab, cooked and cracked, after adding the salt and pepper. Simmer until heated through, then continue as directed.

SERVES 6

❀ In a wide, deep saucepan over medium heat, melt the butter. Add the onions and sauté, stirring occasionally, until tender and translucent, about 10 minutes. Add the jalapeños, nuts (if using), garlic, ginger, and coriander and sauté until heated through and the flavors are blended, about 5 minutes. Add the stock, tomato, coconut milk, saffron and wine, and cilantro and simmer for about 3 minutes to blend the flavors. Add the lemon or lime juice to taste, and season with salt and pepper. Taste and adjust the balance of sweet and sour flavors.

❀ Add the white fish, mussels (discard any that do not close to the touch), and shrimp and simmer until the shrimp are pink, about 3 minutes. Add the scallops during the last 2 minutes and simmer just until the mussels open and the scallops are opaque throughout.

❀ To serve, place 1 cup (5 oz/155 g) rice in each large warmed soup bowl. Ladle the soup into the bowls, dividing the shellfish as evenly as possible and discarding any mussels that did not open. Garnish with the cilantro and coconut. Serve hot.

NUTRITIONAL ANALYSIS PER SERVING: Calories 741 (Kilojoules 3,112); Protein 65 g; Carbohydrates 59 g; Total Fat 25 g; Saturated Fat 11 g; Cholesterol 243 mg; Sodium 705 mg; Dietary Fiber 3 g

Carrot, Apple, and Red Cabbage Slaw with Ginger Vinaigrette

PREP TIME: 30 MINUTES

INGREDIENTS

GINGER VINAIGRETTE

½ cup (2 oz/60 g) sliced peeled fresh ginger

¼ cup (2 fl oz/60 ml) white wine vinegar

¾ cup (6 fl oz/180 ml) vegetable oil such as peanut or canola

1 tablespoon sugar

½ teaspoon salt

½ teaspoon ground pepper

¼ cup (¾ oz/20 g) sesame seeds

3 cups (9 oz/280 g) thinly sliced red cabbage

6 carrots, peeled and julienned

1 tart apple such as pippin or Granny Smith, halved, cored, and thinly sliced

PREP TIP: A mandoline is the ideal tool for cutting the carrots and beets into perfect julienne. You can also use the slicing disk of a food processor for the cabbage, and the julienne or shredding disk to cut the carrots and apples.

This colorful, crisp, refreshing salad is an ideal accompaniment to most Asian-inspired soups. Use chopped, dry-roasted peanuts instead of the sesame seeds, if you prefer. Since the peanuts have already been roasted, they can go straight into the salad without additional toasting. Increase the amount of apple if you like, or leave it out for a more classic slaw. Julienned cooked beets (1½–2 cups/6–8 oz/185–250 g) can be used in place of the carrots.

SERVES 6

❀ To make the ginger vinaigrette, in a food processor or blender, combine the ginger and vinegar and purée. Transfer to a bowl and whisk in the oil, sugar, salt, and pepper. Set aside.

❀ In a small frying pan over medium-high heat, toast the sesame seeds until they pop, about 5 minutes. Set aside.

❀ In a bowl, combine the cabbage, carrots, and apple. Drizzle with the vinaigrette and toss to coat evenly. Top with the sesame seeds and serve immediately.

NUTRITIONAL ANALYSIS PER SERVING: Calories 331 (Kilojoules 1,390); Protein 2 g; Carbohydrates 18 g; Total Fat 29 g; Saturated Fat 5 g; Cholesterol 0 mg; Sodium 225 mg; Dietary Fiber 4 g

Tomato, Cucumber, and Onion Salad with Feta Vinaigrette

PREP TIME: 15 MINUTES

INGREDIENTS

4 beefsteak or assorted heirloom
   tomatoes, thinly sliced

2 cucumbers, halved lengthwise,
   seeded, peeled, and thinly sliced

½ large red (Spanish) onion, sliced
   paper-thin

salt and ground pepper to taste

FETA VINAIGRETTE

1 cup (8 fl oz/250 ml) olive oil

2 tablespoons dried oregano

1 tablespoon finely minced garlic

½ cup (2½ oz/75 g) crumbled feta
   cheese

¼ cup (2 fl oz/60 ml) red wine
   vinegar, or as needed

ground pepper to taste

HEALTHY TIP: For a lighter but still
very flavorful salad, make the dressing without the feta cheese.

When the summer harvest is at its peak, shop your local farmers'
market for heirloom tomatoes. Thin slices of red and green bell
peppers (capsicums) are a nice addition to this plate.

SERVES 6

❀ Arrange the tomato, cucumber, and onion slices on a platter. Sprinkle
lightly with salt and pepper.

❀ To make the vinaigrette, in a blender or food processor, combine the
olive oil, oregano, garlic, feta cheese, vinegar, and pepper. Pulse briefly to
blend. Taste and adjust the seasonings, adding a bit more vinegar if you
like. Spoon over the tomato, cucumber, and onion slices and serve.

NUTRITIONAL ANALYSIS PER SERVING: Calories 423 (Kilojoules 1,777); Protein 5 g;
Carbohydrates 17 g; Total Fat 40 g; Saturated Fat 7 g; Cholesterol 11 mg; Sodium 156 mg;
Dietary Fiber 4 g

Green Bean and New Potato Salad with Salsa Verde

PREP TIME: 20 MINUTES

COOKING TIME: 20 MINUTES

INGREDIENTS

1 lb (500 g) small new potatoes

1 lb (500 g) small green beans

SALSA VERDE

1½ cups (2¼ oz/67 g) finely chopped fresh flat-leaf (Italian) parsley

4–6 tablespoons very finely chopped white onion

¼ cup (2 oz/60 g) capers, rinsed and coarsely chopped

6 cloves garlic, finely minced

4–6 anchovy fillets in olive oil, drained and very finely chopped

⅓ cup (1½ oz/45 g) fine dried bread crumbs

1 cup (8 fl oz/250 ml) extra-virgin olive oil

¼ cup (2 fl oz/60 ml) red wine vinegar or lemon juice

salt and ground pepper to taste

COOKING TIP: When adding the vinegar to the salsa verde, do so gradually, tasting as you go. Vinegars vary in their acidity, and if the one you're using is highly acidic, the sauce may be too sharp. Use lemon juice if you prefer a milder flavor.

Italian *salsa verde,* or green sauce, is also good on cooked beets, carrots, and cauliflower. It will keep for about 1 week in the refrigerator. For a heartier salad, add cooked tuna or salmon fillet or quartered hard-boiled egg to the plate.

SERVES 6

❀ In a saucepan, combine the potatoes with lightly salted water to cover. Bring to a boil, reduce the heat to medium, and simmer, uncovered, until just tender enough to pierce with a fork, about 20 minutes. Drain, let cool, and cut into wedges.

❀ Meanwhile, bring a saucepan three-fourths full of lightly salted water to a boil. Add the green beans, blanch for 3 minutes, and drain. Immediately immerse in cold water to halt the cooking, then drain and pat dry with a kitchen towel.

❀ To make the salsa verde, in a bowl, combine the parsley, onion, capers, garlic, anchovies, and bread crumbs. Whisk in the olive oil, vinegar or lemon juice (see tip), salt, and pepper until blended.

❀ Arrange the potatoes and green beans on a platter. Drizzle on the salsa verde and serve.

NUTRITIONAL ANALYSIS PER SERVING: Calories 455 (Kilojoules 1,911); Protein 5 g; Carbohydrates 27 g; Total Fat 38 g; Saturated Fat 6 g; Cholesterol 2 mg; Sodium 455 mg; Dietary Fiber 4 g

Celery, Mushroom, and Endive Salad

PREP TIME: 20 MINUTES

COOKING TIME: 10 MINUTES

INGREDIENTS

1 cup (4 oz/125 g) walnut halves

DRESSING
½ cup (4 fl oz/125 ml) olive oil

¼ cup (2 fl oz/60 ml) walnut oil

¼ cup (2 fl oz/60 ml) lemon juice

¼ cup (2 fl oz/60 ml) heavy (double) cream

2 teaspoons Dijon mustard (optional)

salt and ground pepper to taste

2 cups (8 oz/250 g) thinly sliced celery

2 cups (6 oz/185 g) thinly sliced cremini mushrooms

3 or 4 heads Belgian endive (chicory/ witloof)

4–5 oz (125–155 g) Gruyère cheese, cut into strips

SERVING TIP: Instead of serving individual salads, line a platter with the dressed endive leaves. Add the cheese to the celery mixture, toss with all the remaining dressing, and spoon over the endive. Scatter the walnuts over the top.

The creamy dressing that coats this salad mellows some of the sharpness of the endive. You can use hazelnuts (filberts) in place of the walnuts, if you like. Toast them as directed until the skins start to loosen, then wrap the warm nuts in a towel and rub off the skins before chopping. Also, substitute hazelnut oil for the walnut oil.

SERVES 6

❀ Preheat an oven to 350°F (180°C). Spread the walnuts on a baking sheet and place in the oven. Toast, stirring occasionally, until lightly colored and fragrant, 8–10 minutes. Remove from the oven and, when cool enough to handle, chop coarsely. Set aside.

❀ To make the dressing, in a small bowl, whisk together the olive and walnut oils, lemon juice, cream, and the mustard, if using. Season with salt and pepper.

❀ In a small bowl, combine the celery and mushrooms. Add about one-third of the dressing and toss to coat evenly.

❀ Trim away the cores of the endives and separate the leaves. Place in a bowl, add about half of the remaining dressing, and toss to coat.

❀ Divide the endive leaves among 6 plates. Top with the celery-mushroom mixture, again dividing evenly. Distribute the cheese strips evenly over the salads, top with the walnuts, drizzle with the remaining dressing, and serve.

NUTRITIONAL ANALYSIS PER SERVING: Calories 503 (Kilojoules 2,113); Protein 11 g; Carbohydrates 8 g; Total Fat 50 g; Saturated Fat 11 g; Cholesterol 37 mg; Sodium 115 mg; Dietary Fiber 3 g

Romaine, Gorgonzola, and Walnut Salad

PREP TIME: 20 MINUTES,
PLUS 15 MINUTES FOR
MARINATING

COOKING TIME: 10 MINUTES

INGREDIENTS

WALNUT VINAIGRETTE

7 tablespoons (3½ fl oz/105 ml) walnut oil

2 tablespoons olive oil

2 tablespoons balsamic vinegar

1 tablespoon sherry vinegar

salt and ground pepper to taste

1 cup (4 oz/125 g) walnuts, preferably halves

3 heads romaine (cos) lettuce, leaves separated and torn into bite-sized pieces

6 small ripe figs, quartered through stem ends (optional)

1 cup (6 oz/185 g) red or black seedless grapes, halved (optional)

2 small pears, quartered, cored, and thinly sliced (optional)

½–⅔ lb (250–315 g) Gorgonzola dolcelatte cheese, at room temperature, broken into bite-sized pieces

PREP TIP: Walnut oil, like all nut oils, is highly perishable. Buy it in small quantities and, once opened, store it in the refrigerator.

Gorgonzola dolcelatte is the sweeter version of the fabulously rich, blue-veined cheese. If you cannot find it at your market, substitute Roquefort or a similar blue cheese. When in season, figs or grapes make a nice addition to the salad. In winter, serve it with wedges of ripe pear.

SERVES 6

❁ Preheat an oven to 350°F (180°C).

❁ To make the walnut vinaigrette, in a bowl, whisk together the walnut and olive oils, balsamic and sherry vinegars, salt, and pepper. Set aside.

❁ Spread the walnuts on a baking sheet and place in the oven. Toast, stirring occasionally, until lightly browned and fragrant, 8–10 minutes. Remove from the oven. Transfer to a small bowl, add 3 tablespoons of the vinaigrette, toss lightly, and let stand for 15 minutes before assembling the salad.

❁ Place the torn romaine in a large bowl. Add the marinated walnuts and drizzle with the remaining vinaigrette. Toss well. Divide among chilled individual plates and top with the figs, grapes, or pears, if using, and the cheese, dividing all the ingredients evenly, and serve.

NUTRITIONAL ANALYSIS PER SERVING: Calories 478 (Kilojoules 2,008); Protein 14 g; Carbohydrates 7 g; Total Fat 46 g; Saturated Fat 12 g; Cholesterol 37 mg; Sodium 599 mg; Dietary Fiber 3 g

Gougères

PREP TIME: 20 MINUTES

COOKING TIME: 50 MINUTES

INGREDIENTS

2 cups (16 fl oz/500 ml) plus 2 table-spoons milk

½ cup (4 oz/125 g) unsalted butter

2 teaspoons salt

2 cups (10 oz/315 g) all-purpose (plain) flour

8 eggs

½ lb (250 g) Emmentaler, Gruyère, or other Swiss-type cheese, finely diced

PREP TIP: To make a festive ring loaf, divide the dough into 2 equal portions. Use a large tablespoon with an oval bowl to scoop out a series of pastry ovals from one portion and form into a ring about 9 inches (23 cm) in diameter. Use a teaspoon to scoop out smaller ovals and use to form a second ring on top of the first. Increase the baking time to 40–45 minutes.

Made from *pâte à choux,* the same dough that is used for cream puffs, these savory cheese pastries are a specialty of France's Burgundy region.

SERVES 6–8

❈ Preheat an oven to 375°F (190°C). Line two baking sheets with parchment (baking) paper.

❈ In a heavy saucepan over high heat, combine the 2 cups (16 fl oz/500 ml) milk, the butter, and salt. Bring to a boil and then add the flour all at once. Reduce the heat to low and stir until the mixture forms a ball and pulls cleanly away from the sides of the pan, about 5 minutes. Remove from the heat. Using an electric mixer set on medium speed, beat in the eggs, one at a time, until the paste is very shiny, about 5 minutes. Fold in three-fourths of the cheese after the last egg has been added.

❈ Using a large tablespoon with an oval bowl, scoop out 2–3-inch (5–7.5-cm) rounds of dough onto the baking sheets, spacing them about 2 inches (5 cm) apart. Brush the rounds with the 2 tablespoons milk and sprinkle with the remaining cheese.

❈ Bake until well puffed and browned, 30–35 minutes. Remove from the oven and let cool for 5 minutes before serving.

NUTRITIONAL ANALYSIS PER SERVING: Calories 528 (Kilojoules 2,218); Protein 24 g; Carbohydrates 35 g; Total Fat 32 g; Saturated Fat 18 g; Cholesterol 324 mg; Sodium 886 mg; Dietary Fiber 1 g

Cheese and Chile Quesadillas

PREP TIME: 30 MINUTES

COOKING TIME: 10 MINUTES

INGREDIENTS

2 large poblano chiles

12 flour tortillas

3 cups (12 oz/375 g) shredded
   Monterey jack cheese

1 cup (3 oz/90 g) finely chopped
   green (spring) onions

salt and ground pepper to taste

vegetable oil

fresh cilantro (fresh coriander)
   leaves, torn

MAKE-AHEAD TIP: The quesadillas
can be assembled ahead of time, covered, and stored on baking sheets in
the refrigerator for up to 8 hours
before cooking.

These could not be simpler to make. If you are in a hurry, use canned green chiles, draining them well. You can also omit the green onions, if you like. Accompany the quesadillas with a bowl of fresh tomato salsa.

SERVES 6

❀ Preheat a broiler (griller). Place the chiles on a baking sheet and broil (grill), turning as needed, until the skins blacken and blister. Do not overcook as they will fall apart. Remove from the broiler, drape loosely with aluminum foil, let cool, then peel away the skins. Cut the chiles in half lengthwise, remove and discard the seeds and stems, and finely dice or cut into long, thin strips.

❀ Place the flour tortillas in a single layer on a work surface. Scatter about ¼ cup (1 oz/30 g) of the cheese over half of each tortilla. Top with the chiles and green onions, dividing them evenly. Sprinkle with salt and pepper. Carefully fold each tortilla in half; do not press down on them or they may crack.

❀ Heat a stove-top grill pan or a heavy frying pan over medium heat. Lightly oil the pan.

❀ Place as many tortillas as will fit on the pan without crowding and weight them down with a pan lid. Cook until golden brown on the first side, about 4 minutes. Carefully flip them over, replace the lid, and cook on the second side until golden and the cheese is melted, about 4 minutes longer. Remove from the griddle or pan and keep warm. Repeat with the remaining filled tortillas.

❀ Cut each filled tortilla in half, sprinkle with the cilantro leaves, and serve at once.

NUTRITIONAL ANALYSIS PER SERVING: Calories 485 (Kilojoules 2,037); Protein 21 g; Carbohydrates 43 g; Total Fat 26 g; Saturated Fat 11 g; Cholesterol 60 mg; Sodium 643 mg; Dietary Fiber 3 g

Mediterranean Egg Salad Sandwich

PREP TIME: 15 MINUTES

COOKING TIME: 10 MINUTES

INGREDIENTS

12 eggs

¼ cup (2 oz/60 g) chopped, drained oil-packed sun-dried tomatoes

¼ cup (1¼ oz/37 g) chopped, pitted Kalamata olives

¾–1 cup (6–8 fl oz/180–250 ml) mayonnaise, preferably homemade

salt and ground pepper to taste

6 slices white, whole-wheat (wholemeal), or coarse country bread (see note)

SERVING TIP: In summer, omit the sun-dried tomatoes and add a slice of ripe tomato to each sandwich instead.

Nearly everyone loves a good egg salad sandwich, especially alongside a bowl of homemade soup. This one is made more interesting with the addition of sun-dried tomatoes and olives. Plain white toast is the classic partner for egg salad, but good whole-wheat (wholemeal) or coarse country bread is an interesting alternative. Serve open-faced, as shown here, or top with another slice of bread and perhaps a lettuce leaf for a more conventional sandwich.

SERVES 6

❋ Fill a large saucepan three-fourths full with lightly salted water and bring to a boil over high heat. Carefully slip the eggs into the water and cover the pan. Reduce the heat to medium and cook for 7–8 minutes. Do not overcook. You want the yolks to be just set in the centers. Drain the eggs, transfer to a bowl, and add cold water to cover. When cool enough to handle, peel and chop coarsely.

❋ In a bowl, combine the chopped eggs, sun-dried tomatoes, olives, and enough mayonnaise to bind the ingredients nicely. Season with salt and pepper. Note that sometimes the tomatoes or olives provide enough salt.

❋ Toast the bread slices. Spread the egg salad on them, dividing it evenly, and serve open-faced sandwiches.

NUTRITIONAL ANALYSIS PER SERVING: Calories 488 (Kilojoules 2,050); Protein 16 g; Carbohydrates 18 g; Total Fat 40 g; Saturated Fat 7 g; Cholesterol 444 mg; Sodium 590 mg; Dietary Fiber 1 g

Buttermilk Chive Biscuits

High rising and incredibly rich, these biscuits are at their best when eaten straight out of the oven. Make them while the soup simmers.

PREP TIME: 25 MINUTES

COOKING TIME: 15 MINUTES

INGREDIENTS

2 cups (10 oz/315 g) all-purpose (plain) flour

2 tablespoons sugar

1½ tablespoons baking powder

½ teaspoon salt

½ cup (4 oz/125 g) chilled unsalted butter, cut into thin slivers

1 whole egg, plus 1 egg yolk (optional)

scant 1 cup (8 fl oz/250 ml) buttermilk, or as needed

¼ cup (⅓ oz/10 g) snipped fresh chives

SERVING TIP: To make cheddar biscuits, add ½ cup (2 oz/60 g) shredded sharp cheddar cheese to the dough after you cut in the butter. Or, for a sweet note, add ½ cup (3 oz/90 g) dried currants with the buttermilk and omit the chives.

MAKES 24 BISCUITS

❋ Preheat an oven to 400°F (200°C). Have ready 2 ungreased baking sheets.

❋ In a bowl, stir together the flour, sugar, baking powder, and salt. Add the butter and, using a pastry blender or 2 knives, cut it in until the mixture resembles coarse meal.

❋ In a measuring pitcher, combine the egg and the egg yolk (if using) and whisk until blended. Add enough buttermilk to measure 1 cup (8 fl oz/ 250 ml). Whisk in the chopped chives. Add the buttermilk mixture to the flour mixture. Using a fork, mix quickly just until the dry ingredients are absorbed.

❋ Turn out the dough onto a heavily floured work surface and knead gently and quickly until the dough is no longer sticky, about 5 minutes. Pat into a square or rectangle ½ inch (12 mm) thick. Dip a round biscuit cutter 3 inches (7.5 cm) in diameter in flour and cut out 24 rounds. Arrange the rounds on ungreased baking sheets about 1 inch (2.5 cm) apart. Bake until golden brown, 12–15 minutes. Remove from the oven and serve hot or warm.

NUTRITIONAL ANALYSIS PER BISCUIT: Calories 92 (Kilojoules 386); Protein 2 g; Carbohydrates 12 g; Total Fat 4 g; Saturated Fat 3 g; Cholesterol 20 mg; Sodium 154 mg; Dietary Fiber 0 g

Ginger Cookies

PREP TIME: 20 MINUTES, PLUS
4 HOURS FOR CHILLING

COOKING TIME: 10 MINUTES

INGREDIENTS

1¼ cups (5 oz/155 g) pecans or (6 oz/
185 g) macadamia nuts

¾ cup plus 2 tablespoons (7 oz/
220 g) unsalted butter, at room
temperature

1¼ cups (10 oz/315 g) sugar, plus
sugar for sprinkling

1 extra-large egg

½ cup (scant 6 oz/185 g) dark
molasses

2½ cups (12½ oz/390 g) all-purpose
(plain) flour

2½ teaspoons baking soda (bicar-
bonate of soda)

1½ tablespoons ground ginger

½ teaspoon ground cinnamon

½ teaspoon salt

¼ teaspoon ground white pepper

¼ cup (½ oz/15 g) minced crystallized ginger

PREP TIP: Double the recipe and
keep extra rolls of the cookie dough
in the freezer for up to 1 month.
When you want to bake them, thaw
partially, slice with a serrated knife,
and bake as directed.

A good, gingery ginger cookie is irresistible. These are a bit chewy and full of flavor. They store well in a covered tin for about 1 week.

MAKES ABOUT 48 COOKIES

❀ Preheat an oven to 350°F (180°C). Spread the nuts on a baking sheet and toast until lightly browned and fragrant, 8–10 minutes. Remove from the oven, let cool, and chop coarsely; set aside.

❀ In a bowl, using an electric mixer preferably fitted with a paddle attachment, beat together the butter and the 1¼ cups (10 oz/315 g) sugar until creamy, about 5 minutes. Add the egg and beat until fluffy, about 5 minutes. Then add the molasses and beat to combine.

❀ In another bowl, sift together the flour, baking soda, ground ginger, cinnamon, salt, and white pepper. Add the flour mixture to the butter mixture and beat until well mixed, 2–3 minutes. Stir in the crystallized ginger and nuts until evenly distributed.

❀ Lightly flour a work surface. Divide the dough into 2 equal portions. Form each portion into a log about 1½ inches (4 cm) in diameter. Wrap tightly in plastic wrap and refrigerate until well chilled, at least 4 hours or for up to 2 days.

❀ Preheat an oven to 325°F (165°C). Line the bottoms of 2 baking sheets with parchment (baking) paper. Using a sharp knife, cut each log into slices ⅛ inch (3 mm) thick. Arrange the slices on the prepared baking sheets, spacing them about 1 inch (2.5 cm) apart.

❀ Bake until golden, 8–10 minutes. Remove from the oven, transfer to a rack, and sprinkle with sugar. Let cool.

NUTRITIONAL ANALYSIS PER COOKIE: Calories 113 (Kilojoules 475); Protein 1 g Carbohydrates 15 g; Total Fat 6 g; Saturated Fat 2 g; Cholesterol 14 mg; Sodium 94 mg; Dietary Fiber 0 g

Mixed Fruit Gratin

PREP TIME: 10 MINUTES

COOKING TIME: 10 MINUTES

INGREDIENTS

8 cups (2 lb/1 kg) mixed stemmed
    strawberries, raspberries, and
    blueberries or peeled, pitted,
    and sliced peaches and whole
    blackberries

1½ cups (12 fl oz/375 ml) sour cream

3 tablespoons milk or half-and-half

¼ cup (2 oz/60 g) granulated sugar

½–⅔ cup (3½–5 oz/105–155 g) firmly
    packed brown sugar, or as needed

MAKE-AHEAD TIP: This dish can be
completely assembled except for the
brown sugar topping and refrigerated
up to 4 hours in advance. Bring to
room temperature before sprinkling
with the brown sugar and slipping
under the broiler.

This makes a dramatic ending to a simple soup meal and tastes more complicated to make than it actually is. Use seasonal fruits that are at their peak. Pitted and sliced nectarines can be used in place of the peaches.

SERVES 6

❀ Preheat a broiler (griller).

❀ If using strawberries, cut into quarters or halves, depending upon the size of the berries. Place the mixed berries or the peaches and black-berries in the bottom of a 9-by-13-inch (23-by-33-cm) flameproof baking dish. In a bowl, whisk together the sour cream, the milk or half-and-half, and the granulated sugar. Spoon the mixture evenly over the fruit. Sprinkle the brown sugar evenly over the top.

❀ Place the dish under the broiler about 4 inches (10 cm) from the heat source. Broil (grill) until the brown sugar melts and bubbles, 8–10 minutes.

❀ Remove from the broiler and serve at once.

NUTRITIONAL ANALYSIS PER SERVING: Calories 326 (Kilojoules 1369); Protein 3 g; Carbohydrates 53 g; Total Fat 13 g; Saturated Fat 8 g; Cholesterol 26 mg; Sodium 46 mg; Dietary Fiber 5 g

Lemon-Scented Ricotta

PREP TIME: 10 MINUTES, PLUS
24 HOURS FOR CHILLING

INGREDIENTS

2 cups (1 lb/500 g) ricotta cheese

1⅓ cups (11 oz/345 g) sugar

⅓ cup (3 fl oz/80 ml) dark rum

2 tablespoons finely grated lemon
zest, plus shredded zest for garnish

2 tablespoons lemon juice

2 cups (8 oz/250 g) berries such as
raspberries or sliced strawberries,
or 2 or 3 peaches, peeled, pitted,
and sliced

This is so easy, you'll want to serve it often. You will need very fresh and creamy ricotta. Look for it at an Italian delicatessen or at a food store with a well-stocked cheese department. Sugar cookies are perfect for serving alongside.

SERVES 4–6

❀ In a bowl, combine the ricotta cheese, sugar, rum, lemon zest, and lemon juice. Using an electric mixer, beat until fluffy and well blended, about 5 minutes.

❀ Spoon into ramekins or custard cups, cover, and refrigerate until set, about 24 hours.

❀ Serve chilled with the berries or peach slices alongside.

NUTRITIONAL ANALYSIS PER SERVING: Calories 458 (Kilojoules 1924); Protein 11 g; Carbohydrates 71 g; Total Fat 12 g; Saturated Fat 8 g; Cholesterol 46 mg; Sodium 78 mg; Dietary Fiber 2 g

Amaretti-Stuffed Baked Peaches

PREP TIME: 20 MINUTES

COOKING TIME: 25 MINUTES

INGREDIENTS

¾ cup (3 oz/90 g) sliced (flaked) almonds

6 ripe peaches

14 amaretti

¼ cup (2 oz/60 g) sugar

½ teaspoon ground ginger

½ cup (4 oz/125 g) unsalted butter, cut into 8 equal slices

½ cup (4 fl oz/125 ml) sweet Marsala, white wine, or orange juice

MAKE-AHEAD TIP: The peaches can be assembled up to 6 hours in advance and refrigerated until baking time.

Amaretti, Italy's wonderful almond-flavored macaroons, are easy to find at your local Italian market and they make a wonderful filling for baked peaches. Serve with peach, almond, or vanilla ice cream, or with whipped cream scented with vanilla or almond extract (essence).

SERVES 6

❀ Preheat an oven to 350°F (180°C). Spread the almonds on a baking sheet and toast, shaking the pan or stirring occasionally, until lightly browned and fragrant, about 10 minutes. Remove from the oven and let cool.

❀ Raise the oven temperature to 375°F (190°C). Lightly butter a baking dish in which the peaches, once halved, will fit in a single layer, without crowding.

❀ Bring a saucepan three-fourths full of water to a boil. Working in batches, carefully slip the peaches into the boiling water for about 1 minute, then remove with a slotted spoon. When cool enough to handle, peel away the skins. Cut each peach in half through the stem end and remove and discard the pit. Place the peach halves, hollow sides up, in the prepared baking dish.

❀ In a food processor, combine the amaretti, ½ cup (2 oz/60 g) of the toasted almonds, sugar, and ginger. Pulse a few times until the cookies are crumbled. Add the butter and process until a paste forms. Mound the almond paste in the centers of the peach halves, dividing evenly.

❀ Bake, basting the peaches with a little Marsala, white wine, or orange juice, until tender and golden, about 25 minutes. Remove from the oven, transfer to individual plates, and garnish with the remaining ¼ cup (1 oz/30 g) toasted almonds.

NUTRITIONAL ANALYSIS PER SERVING: Calories 375 (Kilojoules 1575); Protein 4 g; Carbohydrates 38 g; Total Fat 22 g; Saturated Fat 10 g; Cholesterol 43 mg; Sodium 11 mg; Dietary Fiber 3 g

Dried-Fruit Compote

PREP TIME: 5 MINUTES, PLUS
4 HOURS FOR SOAKING
AND CHILLING

COOKING TIME: 45 MINUTES

INGREDIENTS

1½ lb (750 g) assorted dried fruits
such as pitted prunes, apricots,
pears, apples, and raisins

5–6 cups (40–48 fl oz/1.25–1.5 l)
water or Riesling, Moscato, or
other sweet wine

1 cup (8 oz/250 g) sugar, or to taste

2 lemon zest strips

1 small cinnamon stick

MAKE-AHEAD TIP: The compote can
be prepared up to 5 days in advance
if covered and stored in the refrigerator. Bring to room temperature
before serving.

In the winter, when a wide variety of fresh fruits is hard to find,
this compote of dried fruits is a wonderful alternative. Serve
with or without a pitcher of heavy (double) cream. The dried
fruits are also delicious cooked in a fragrant tea such as black
currant, peach, or ginger.

SERVES 6

❀ Place the dried fruits in a bowl and add enough water or wine to cover
(about 3 cups/24 fl oz/750 ml). Cover and let stand at room temperature
for 2 hours.

❀ Transfer the soaked fruits and their liquid to a nonaluminum saucepan
and add enough water or wine to cover by about 2 inches (5 cm). Then
add the sugar, lemon zest, and cinnamon stick and bring to a boil over
high heat. Reduce the heat to low and simmer, uncovered, until the
fruits are tender, 30–45 minutes. Remove from the heat and let cool,
then cover and refrigerate until chilled, about 2 hours.

❀ Bring to room temperature before serving.

NUTRITIONAL ANALYSIS PER SERVING: Calories 419 (Kilojoules 1760); Protein 3 g;
Carbohydrates 110 g; Total Fat 1 g; Saturated Fat 0 g; Cholesterol 0 g; Sodium 28 mg; Dietary
Fiber 6 g

HERBS

In both their fresh and dried forms, herbs add their flavor and fragrance to countless soups. Because the intensity of dried herbs dissipates over time, buy them in small quantities, seal them in jars, and store in a cool, dry place. Rub dried herbs between your fingertips or your thumb and palm before use to release more of their essential oils. To store fresh herbs, place the stem ends in a glass of water like a bouquet of flowers or wrap them in damp paper towels in a plastic bag and refrigerate.

BAY LEAF

The dried whole leaves of the bay laurel tree have a deep, pungent flavor that imparts an aromatic accent to soups. Seek out the Turkish variety, which has a milder, sweeter flavor than bay leaves from California. The tough, sharp-edged leaves are generally removed from soups before serving.

CHIVES

Used most often in soups as a garnish added to individual servings, chives provide an onionlike flavor without the bite. Mild and sweet, they are at their best when raw, as cooking diminishes their flavor. Steer clear of bottled dried chives, which also lack the taste of the fresh herb.

CILANTRO

Also known as fresh coriander and Chinese parsley, cilantro has flat, frilly leaves that resemble those of flat-leaf (Italian) parsley. Its flavor is astringent and slightly grassy, with a hint of spice. It is widely used in Asian and Latin American soups.

DILL

This feathery herb has a sprightly, almost sweet taste and delicate aroma that is best appreciated when at its freshest—that is, when the leaves and stems are bright green. Most often, it is added to soups as a garnish before serving.

PARSLEY, FLAT-LEAF

Also known as Italian parsley, this variety of the widely popular fresh herb, native to southern Europe, has a more pronounced flavor than the common curly type, making it preferable as a seasoning. With its pleasantly grassy flavor, parsley, particularly in the form of its stems, forms part of the flavor base of many soups. Flat-leaf parsley also makes an attractive garnish.

THYME

One of the most important culinary herbs of European kitchens, thyme delivers a light fragrance and subtle flavor to nearly all savory foods. It goes particularly well with meats, poultry, and seafood, as well as vegetables and mild cheeses. Fresh thyme sprigs are an essential seasoning element for classic soup stocks.

CREMINI

Earthy brown caps, firmer texture, and richer flavor distinguish these cultivated mushrooms, the immature form of the popular portobello mushroom, from the more commonplace and similarly shaped white mushrooms.

PORCINI

Prized for their tender texture and rich flavor, porcini are found fresh in summer and autumn. At other times, dried porcini may be found in Italian delicatessens and specialty-food stores. They are also known by the French as *cèpes*.

WHITE

This most common cultivated mushroom variety, white mushrooms are abundant and inexpensive, and available year-round. Their flavor is somewhat nutty and creamy when raw. When sliced or chopped and cooked in butter or oil, their flavor intensifies and becomes earthy and rich.

OLIVE OIL

Olive oil is an essential ingredient in many soups, particularly those of Mediterranean origin. Some olive oils are spicy with a peppery kick, others buttery and mellow; in every case, they reflect the trees that produced the olives, the land, and the growing conditions. Those labeled "extra virgin" have been extracted from ripe olives on the first pressing by pressure alone; they have the fullest flavor and are best suited for use in dressings and as a condiment or seasoning. Oils labeled "pure" are blended and better suited to general cooking purposes.

PANCETTA

A specialty of the Emilia-Romagna region in northern Italy. Pancetta is the same belly cut of pork as bacon, but unlike bacon, pancetta is only salt-cured, not smoked. Used as part of an aromatic base, pancetta brings a rich undertone of flavor to soup. Fried and crumbled, it makes a crisp, savory garnish.

SPICES

Aromatic seeds, berries, buds, roots, and bark are all used as spices, and are indispensable flavor-enhancers for soups of all kinds. Crushing them releases their essential oils, so buy whole spices whenever possible and grind them as needed in an electric spice mill or in a mortar with a pestle. When only ground spices are available, buy them in small quantities and replenish your supply when their flavor noticeably diminishes.

ALLSPICE

This sweet Caribbean spice, sold ground or as whole dried berries, is named for its flavor, which resembles a blend of cinnamon, cloves, and nutmeg.

CAYENNE PEPPER

Prized for its heat and bright red color, this fine powder is ground from the dried cayenne chile.

CLOVES

These dried flower buds of an evergreen tree native to Southeast Asia have a rich, highly aromatic flavor. They may be used whole or ground in both savory and sweet recipes.

CORIANDER SEEDS

These tiny, lightly ridged seeds are actually the dried ripe fruit of the fresh herb cilantro. The seeds have a mild fragrance and flavor and are often ground and used as a seasoning in Middle Eastern and Indian cuisines.

SAFFRON

It takes the hairlike stigmas from more than 75,000 blossoms of a variety of crocus to yield just 1 pound (500 g) of this golden-hued, richly perfumed spice, one of the world's most expensive. However, just the smallest pinch of the dried stigmas, generally known as saffron "threads," is enough to give a dish a bright golden color and heady aroma. Avoid buying saffron that has been ground into a powder, a process that not only makes its flavor dissipate more rapidly but also allows for the possibility of adulterating the coveted spice.

TURMERIC

This popular Asian spice comes from a rhizome (underground stem) and has a mildly pungent, earthy flavor. Turmeric lends its bright yellow-orange color to whatever it seasons.

TOMATOES

Tomatoes add savory-sweet flavor and rich body to soups. For the best taste and texture, seek out those that have ripened on the vine beneath the summer sun. When vine-ripened tomatoes are not available, a good year-round choice is the egg-shaped plum (Roma) variety. Good-quality canned tomatoes are also an excellent alternative to fresh tomatoes in many soups.

To peel a tomato, using a small, sharp knife, cut out its core and score a shallow X in the skin on the opposite end. Immerse in boiling water for about 20 seconds, then transfer to a bowl of ice water. The skins should peel off easily, either with your fingertips or with the assistance of the knife. To seed a tomato, cut it in half horizontally and use a fingertip or the handle of a small spoon to scoop out the seed sacs. Then, using a small, sharp knife, cut the seedless pulp into pieces of the desired size and shape.

VINEGARS

Vinegar can lend a sharp, intense edge of flavor to soups and their accompaniments. The word derives from the French *vin aigre,* or "sour wine," a reference to the secondary fermentation that occurs in wine to produce vinegar. While wine is, in fact, the source of many vinegars, a number of popular vinegars are made from grains and other fruits.

BALSAMIC VINEGAR

Made from cooked and reduced grape juice rather than wine, this highly prized Italian vinegar is aged for many years in a progression of ever-smaller barrels made of different woods. The result is a vinegar of almost syruplike consistency, with a complex and intense flavor sufficiently sweet to make it as suitable a sauce for berries as it is for use in dressings or other savory dishes. The words *aceto balsamico tradizionale* on the label indicate that the vinegar was made in Italy according to traditional artisan methods.

RED WINE VINEGAR

Red wine vinegar possesses much of the robust character of the wine from which it is made. As with wine, the more full-flavored vinegars are best paired with more assertive, heartier foods.

SHERRY VINEGAR

A deep caramel color and rich, full flavor characterize a fine sherry vinegar. Made from the Spanish fortified wine from which it takes its name, the best sherry vinegar is aged in the same wooden casks used to produce the wine, which impart their own unique flavor.

INDEX

ACKNOWLEDGMENTS

The publishers would like to thank the following people and associations for their generous support and assistance in producing this book: Ken DellaPenta, Jennifer Hanson, Hill Nutrition Associates, Sharilyn Hovind, Lisa Lee, and Cecily Upton.

The following kindly lent props for photography: Fillamento, Williams-Sonoma, and Pottery Barn, San Francisco, CA; the Gardener, Berkeley, CA. The photographer would like to thank Richard Atwood for generously sharing his home with us for our location setting. We would also like to thank Chromeworks and ProCamera, San Francisco, CA, and FUJI Film for their generous support of this project. Special acknowledgment goes to Daniel Yearwood for the beautiful backgrounds and surface treatments.